A Mother's Perspective

From Joy to Anguish and Back Again

By Kevin Stine

Copyright © 2021 Kevin Stine. All rights reserved.
Published by PurposeHouse Publishing, Columbia, Maryland.
Printed in USA

No part of this publication may be reproduced or distributed in any form or by any means, or stored in a database or retrieval system, without the prior written permission of the author.

ISBN: 978-0-692-03295-4

Scripture quotations taken from The Holy Bible, New International Version® NIV ® Copyright © 2011 by Biblica, Inc. TM. Used by permission. All rights reserved worldwide.

Scripture quotations taken from the (NASB®) New American Standard Bible®, Copyright © 2020 by The Lockman Foundation. Used by permission. All rights reserved. www.lockman.org."

Contents

Introduction	1
Chapter 1: The Hope	9
Post-Pentecost	9
Chapter 2: The Crucifixion	15
At the cross	15
That Evening - At Home	22
The Next Day - The Sabbath	37
Chapter 3: The Resurrection	53
The First Day of the Week	53
At the Tomb	55
Reflection	60
Stories of Jesus Sightings	79
Chapter 4: The Ascension	89
Marriage	91
Messianic Prophecies	100
Looking Back at the Cross	109
Stories from the Disciples	114
Chapter 5: The Holy Spirit	135
Epilogue	141

Introduction

Considering Mary was the mother of Jesus, there isn't very much written about her in the Bible. That's understandable, given that the Bible is written about Jesus. However, short of being impregnated by the Holy Spirit and raising the Son of God, she likely led a life strewn with challenges and hardships that most people can relate to or at least understand, even if they haven't experienced them.

The Bible makes it clear that Jesus suffered on our behalf. He was perfect, but out of his perfection, he suffered torment for us to know God because of our sins. It was through his selfless life, death, and resurrection that we can be assured of our salvation, as long as we believe in him. That is the good news—the best news imaginable. We don't seem to understand or don't typically want to accept that those who are Christ's followers are also going to have difficult times. Just because our Lord suffered does not mean we will not suffer. In fact, the opposite is true. However, we can rest assured because *"we are hard pressed on every side, but not crushed; perplexed, but not in despair; persecuted, but not abandoned; struck down, but not destroyed."*[1] No matter how difficult the situation, God is there for us, helping us. If we understand this, we should also understand that when we suffer as followers of Christ, we can still do good for others. Those who seek and follow the Lord Jesus may not always be able to see the big picture, but we are called to be committed—to be obedient. That seems to be what was demonstrated through the life of Mary, the mother of Jesus. She modeled a life of obedience, even during difficult times.

Early on in the life of Jesus, we are told that Mary, the mother of Jesus, *"treasured up all these things and pondered them in her heart."*[2] Over about a year, Mary went from being told that she (a virgin) would have a baby boy, to having the baby (in a manger), to being visited by shepherds with an amazing story, and

---

[1] 2 Corinthians 4:8-9 New International Version (NIV)
[2] Luke 2:19 NIV

then being told her child would be God's salvation. Through all of this, what did Mary ponder? What thoughts went through her mind? What did she think—not only during this initial time in the life of Jesus, but also what else did the mother of our Lord and Savior ponder throughout the life, death, resurrection, and ascension of her son?

Historical documents do not seem to have recorded Mary's thoughts and ponderings. Still, with a bit of imagination, we can develop some realistic ideas of what she may have thought about the events in her son's life. This story starts with Mary recently experiencing Pentecost, the coming of the Holy Spirit, and having full knowledge of who her son is—the Messiah—the Son of God Almighty. From there, she flashes back to Calvary and the extreme anguish she suffered as a mother. Then, through a series of questions, memories, and experiences, she takes us on her journey to Pentecost.

The seasons of Mary's life include the cross on which they killed her son. We didn't hear about Mary grieving, but how could she not have grieved? She "lost" her son. What mother wouldn't grieve? Whether the prophet Zechariah was talking specifically about Jesus' mother or people in general, he stated, *"They will look on me, the one they have pierced, and they will mourn for him as one mourns for an only child, and grieve bitterly for him as one grieves for a firstborn son."*[3] As any mother would, Mary mourned and grieved over her son's death; the pain of Jesus' unjust death pierced her heart like knives.

Not only was there suffering at the cross, which would have been the ultimate grief for a mother to experience, but Jesus' family endured much over the years. It would be easy to assume that being part of the family of God's Son, one would have a privileged life, but that would be a false assumption. God did not spare his son or son's family from a life of suffering. It should be clear that if God

---

[3] Zechariah 12:10 NIV

would not spare his son from a life of suffering, he will not spare us that life. That may not bring comfort to a person in a grieving situation, but the good news states there is hope beyond this life, a hope filled with much joy. We will not fully see that joy played out this side of eternity, but we can rest assured that joy is coming. Not only do we have a Savior who suffered and as such understands our suffering, but he also told us that when he returns, there will be much joy, no more grieving. When we see Jesus, we will rejoice. No one will be able to take that joy away. Until it is our time to experience total joy at the Second Coming of Jesus, let's consider one mother's potential response to repeated anguish. She experienced being scared, fleeing for her life, thinking she lost her son, and grieving the death of her nephew and husband. Let's consider how she went from agonizing over her son's death and then finally to the ultimate joy of experiencing his resurrection from the dead and truly realizing he is the Son of God! Mary experienced a lot of grief and heartache, especially considering she was a woman who found favor with God, but she also experienced tremendous joy.

Christians experience hardships and grief at times, even when we actively seek God and fully believe we are obeying him. Hopefully, this book will encourage readers, even in those times of suffering, that God is in control, that he has a bigger plan than we can imagine. It doesn't mean it won't hurt during those times, as Mary surely experienced. After all, God had his Son sacrificed for each of us. That action caused pain and suffering in many ways for Jesus, his family, and his friends. No one escaped the suffering. During that suffering, Jesus' family and friends could not see the big picture until they experienced Jesus' resurrection from the dead. Likewise, it is not possible for us to fully know why we experience various forms of grief, at least not until Jesus returns at his Second Coming. What we do have is the promise of his return. At that point, we will experience pure joy. Until then, we are to remain obedient, and we can remain confident that *"God so loved the world that he gave his one and only Son, that whoever believes in him shall not perish but have eternal life."*[4]

Let's look at the life of Mary to see an example of someone seeking God while enduring many challenges and hardships, continuing with a life of obedience, and in the end, rejoicing with the joy that is available only through Christ. With Mary in view as our example, we can see that even when everything around us seems to be falling apart, we can have the assurance that God has a master plan.

---

[4] John 3:16 NIV

Chapter 1: The Hope

Post-Pentecost

God has blessed me with a unique experience, which allows me to lay claim to something no one else can say or will ever be able to say. It has nothing to do with what I did or who I was. God simply chose me to be the mother of Jesus—Jesus, the Christ, the Messiah, the Son of God.

The mother of Jesus. That's a rather big deal, or should I say a rather large blessing. However, it was not always recognized as a blessing, especially when we were going through some difficult times, and there were some difficult times. The life of raising the Son of God was full of ups and downs. At this point in my life, it's easy for me to look back at all the events and see God's hand at work, but it wasn't always easy to recognize God's workmanship during the difficult times. Now, based on that previous experience, I am convinced there are going to be even more difficult times and hardships, but I can face them with more certainty than ever that God has a plan, a perfect plan of love, forgiveness, and salvation.

As God chose the Israelites to be his people, he chose me to carry his Son. He created everyone, and he could have chosen any people group on the earth to be his chosen nation, but he chose Israel. Likewise, he could have chosen anyone to carry and raise his Son, but he chose me. It would be easy to ask why God put me on this mission or why God allowed so much pain and grief in my life while being a part of his plan. These are very legitimate questions—questions that may or may not have understandable answers within my lifetime. As I already mentioned, I'm not even sure that all the ups and downs are over. What I do know is that God is with me, he has a plan, and he will see it through.

It was an extreme honor to be the mother of Jesus, but I really don't think I fully comprehended the magnitude of the task or the child I was raising, let alone the full breadth of his infinite nature. Through Jesus' death, resurrection, and ascension, as well as the indwelling of the Holy Spirit that came upon all his followers, I gained a better understanding of who Jesus is—so much more understanding than all the years of being with him as his mother. It is quite clear that I didn't fully grasp all that Jesus is or all that he taught. It's most likely that no one, not even his disciples, really understood him.

Following his resurrection from the tomb, Jesus made quite an impact on the lives of his disciples. They now have a boldness about their beliefs and their teachings about the hope we have in Jesus. The disciples each have a different approach, but I'll tell you, when John starts talking about eternal life for anyone who believes in Jesus, I start to cry—good tears. All we have to do is to believe in Jesus, and we get eternal life. It's that simple, but most of us (especially me) didn't understand it when Jesus lived with us.

It's only been a short while since Jesus' ascension, and I'm learning more and more all the time. Most of my learning comes from the disciples, as this teaching isn't coming out of the synagogues yet. The chief priests and Pharisees are still trying to stop "The Way" from progressing. I don't believe they will be successful at that attempt, but they are trying very hard. There's one particularly zealous Pharisee named Saul, who is making life very difficult for those who believe in the resurrection of Jesus. He may even be the force behind the imprisonment and killing of many followers of Jesus. I am constantly praying to God that he puts a stop to the actions of Saul. Jesus taught that we are to *"love your enemies and pray for those who persecute you."*[5] That is surely a hard teaching, especially when considering someone like Saul who is killing our Christian brothers and sisters. There is still so much to learn regarding Jesus' teachings.

From my personal experience, criticizing or condemning those who haven't believed yet is not a good approach. After all, it is a rather remarkable story of hope and faith. I've not always understood this hope that we now have in Jesus, the hope of

---

[5] Matthew 5:44 NIV

eternal life he promises to those who love him and seek him. I surely didn't understand this hope on that horrific day at the cross. When thinking back to that day, I remember that there wasn't the smallest bit of hope within my being.

Chapter 2: The Crucifixion

At the cross

I can hardly breathe.

My knees are weak. I don't have the strength to stand.

It just feels like they ripped a part of me away. They did!

They tore my son away from me. They just killed my son—my firstborn.

Never could there be anything more excruciatingly painful to watch. I couldn't even watch all of it. I had to close my eyes and turn my head away at times. My heart just broke.

I can't imagine how painful it was for him. What sort of beast could drive those nails into someone's hands and feet, all the while hearing their screams of pain? Those screams were horrific, as they hammered nails through his hands and feet—not just nails but large spikes! Covering my ears with my hands could not block that sound. It had to be the most horrible sound imaginable.

How is a mother supposed to watch or listen to such treatment of her son?

The horrible sights and sounds didn't stop with them nailing him to the cross. When they stood the cross up, his entire body weight pulled on the nails in his hands and feet, tearing his flesh. Then, after he seemed to lose the strength needed to support his weight, I could see and hear his shoulders pop from their sockets. It sent chills down my spine; it was so painful to watch. I didn't want to be there, but I couldn't leave my son.

No one deserves such treatment. The pain must have been so intense. It was the first I ever heard him question God: *"My God, my God, why have you forsaken me?"*[6] Not in all his years did he

---

[6] Mark 15:34 NIV

ever question God—ever! The pain must have been so intense for him to question God.

It didn't take long before he struggled to breathe. He was gasping for each breath. While struggling for his final breaths, he still had strength enough to forgive them—his executioners. The crowd could hear him say, *"Father, forgive them, for they do not know what they are doing."*[7] How could anyone accuse him of anything worthy of death? Even on the cross, he was willing to forgive and love others up until his final breath. Who else would do that? How could anyone blame and execute someone of such godly character?

Not only did my son not deserve to die, he surely didn't deserve to be killed by the most inhumane method known—crucifixion. Why did they do it?

Even before they nailed him to the cross, it was obvious that they had tortured him. Who knows what they did to him

---

[7] Luke 23:34 NIV

throughout the night? All I could see was his bloodied body, seemingly in pain with every step he took. They wouldn't allow me to go to him, to hug him, to tell him I loved him. They just treated him like a murderer.

It all started at 9:00 in the morning, and by 3:00 in the afternoon, he took his final breath. For six hours, he endured the pain and the mockery of the cross. For six hours, I had to watch my son go through this horrific ordeal. I had never watched a crucifixion before. And now, I never want to again. People were watching strictly for entertainment. Why would anyone want to do that? What's wrong with people?

Some people in the crowd claimed that one of the centurions who witnessed the day's events was convinced that Jesus was the Son of God. Well, that's fine. But isn't it a little too late to make that statement now, now that Jesus is dead!

I was just beside myself, not knowing what to do. What just happened? How do I go on with life? First, my beloved husband,

Joseph, died. The experiences we had together were amazing, especially the conditions under which we married and the conditions under which Jesus was born—in the feeding trough for farm animals. Now, they are both gone. Why? What did I do to deserve this?

From the cross, Jesus told me that John is my son and that I am John's mother. What sense does that make? Why did he bother with such a statement while he hung on the cross? He probably had so much love and compassion for others that even through the intense pain he suffered, his very nature still showed his extreme love for others. He also taught us that we should not worry about anything. As an aging widow, it would be natural for me to worry, but having someone like John looking after me would surely help minimize that worry. But why would Jesus consider this while he hung there on the cross? I am very confused about all that is going on. Less than 24 hours ago, life was normal, with no indication of such events about to happen.

John sure took Jesus' words seriously. He invited me to stay with his family, saying that is what Jesus would want him to do. I had to consider his offer seriously, but what I really wanted was for Jesus to be with me that night, in my own home. And still, I don't want to be anywhere else. I don't want to do anything different. I want everything to be the same as it was. I don't have the strength to go through another hardship.

Before considering where I'm spending my aging years, I've got to worry about where to place Jesus' body. Tomorrow is the Sabbath, so we must prepare his body before then. It all happened so quickly that we had nowhere to lay his body, no gravesite. Why would we have a place for him? After all, just five days ago, he rode a donkey through the streets of Jerusalem, with people laying coats and palms on the ground in front of him—a celebration. They were so excited to see him. How could that have turned into this situation?

Where am I going to place his body?

Who is Joseph of Arimathea? He was bold enough to approach Pilate to request to have Jesus' body. It is not just anyone who can approach Pilate. He must be someone of some importance, so why is he taking Jesus' body? He didn't ask for my approval. Who am I? Just a woman, apparently with no value. Not only did he take Jesus' body, but before he placed the body in his tomb, he carefully wrapped it in cloths. He properly cared for Jesus' body. He was so kind. Apparently, Joseph is a member of the Council—a member of the Council that condemned Jesus. So, why would a member of the Council take proper care of Jesus' body? Absolutely nothing is making sense to me.

Because tomorrow is the Sabbath, we cannot do any more for Jesus at this time. After the Sabbath, the other women and I can prepare spices and perfumes that we can apply to Jesus' body on the first day of the week.

It is still unbelievable that someone took care of Jesus' burial. What a blessing at such an awful time.

That Evening - At Home

I am so lost and confused, and I hurt so badly. Will I ever understand what has happened? Will it ever make sense? How could it possibly make sense? It was a completely senseless act!

This day is going to haunt me forever!

Less than one week ago, the crowds were praising Jesus. They would have done anything for him. They loved him. Now I'm being told the crowd changed their tune and chose Barabbas, a known murderer, to be released in exchange for Jesus to be crucified. How could that have happened? What were the people thinking? From shouting "hosanna" one day to shouting "crucify him" less than one week later. I am shocked beyond words!

After deciding to crucify him, they mocked him by placing a crown of thorns on his head, making him bleed. The blood could still be seen running down his face as they walked him to The Skull—the place where they killed him. I so wanted to wipe the blood from his face, to hold and comfort him, but I wasn't allowed to be near him.

I wish no one had told me they also flogged him—ripping flesh from his body. Those barbarian soldiers apparently seemed to enjoy it. How could any human do that to another human? It just makes me sick hearing about what they did to Jesus before they killed him. It sounds like they started the mockery of a trial and the torture before anyone had even told me he had been arrested. It all happened so fast. The first I could see him was on the road to Golgotha, where I saw he was made to carry his own cross. He could barely stand as it was. I was so glad when they made Simon of Cyrene carry the cross for him. My son could barely walk, even without carrying the cross. The sight just made me weep uncontrollably.

When they reached Golgotha, they offered him wine with myrrh before driving the nails into his hands. Was that to help numb his feelings? They didn't care how he felt. They continued laughing and mocking him while hanging a sign that read, *"King of the Jews."*[8]

Is it possible for me to ever get the sights and sounds of the day from my head? I don't know how many times the events of the cross keep flashing before me, and it has only been a few hours. Over and over, I see them driving the nails into his hands and feet, and the pain that could be seen on his face is unbearable. If I close my eyes, I can still hear his screams echoing through my head. That sight and sound will forever be etched in my head. It is the most horrible thing. How can I possibly live with that vision for the rest of my life? In fact, the sights and sounds from the entire day are permanently planted in my mind. After he hung there for a while, there was the sound of his joints popping while becoming dislocated from the sheer weight of his body hanging from them. First, his shoulders popped, then his elbows and wrists. After that, you could see his arms stretching longer and longer. My whole body

---

[8] Matthew 27:37 NIV

shuddered in shock and pain at what he could be going through at that moment. How can I ever get this image out of my mind? I can also still hear him struggling to breathe, such painful breathing. You could tell it was painful for him even to breathe. Oh, that sound was just horrible! And the mockery continued in so many ways. They made him hang there completely naked. How humiliating! They were like animals—absolutely no humanity among them.

It has only been a few hours since I heard Jesus' last words, *"It is finished."*[9] His head went limp. His body was lifeless. It was a mother's worst nightmare: the death of her child and such a horrific death. My legs just collapsed. They could not support my weight. The absolute worst had just happened. The soldier's announcement wasn't required; I knew my son was dead. I just dropped to my knees. I can't stop thinking about it. The same questions keep racing through my mind:

Why? Why was he even arrested in the first place?

---

[9] John 19:30 NIV

Why did his disciple and friend, Judas Iscariot, betray him? What did Jesus ever do to him that caused such betrayal? Jesus loved each of his disciples. He loved everyone!

Why didn't Peter try to save Jesus instead of denying that he even knew Jesus—three times? What sort of friend was he? Did he really love Jesus, as he claimed? Doesn't a friend go to the rescue of another friend?

Why did the soldiers have to mock him so? He loved everyone. Why did they feel the need to mock him, giving him a purple robe and a crown made of thorns and spitting on him? Even the others who were crucified with him mocked him. As they hung there, even they felt the need to mock a man who loved more than anyone I've ever known.

I keep asking myself, over and over, how could the crowds be waving palm branches one day while shouting, *"Hosanna to the*

Son of David!"[10] and just a few days later exclaiming, *"crucify him"?*[11] Oh, I am just numb at all of this.

Did they really release a murderer? Now we will worry about this man Barabbas walking about our town, worrying about who he will kill next.

Why were they casting lots—rolling dice for his clothes? He wasn't even dead. They didn't really want his clothes. It was just another way of mocking him while he hung on the cross, clearly in his sight of view. They had no feelings, no compassion.

Oh, why did they have to "spear" him? It was obvious he was already dead, so why did the soldier have to thrust that spear into Jesus' side? It almost seemed like he enjoyed it. Anyone could see that Jesus was already dead. It felt like they stabbed me with that sword. It just cut right through to my innermost being.

---

[10] Matthew 21:9 NIV
[11] Mark 15:13 NIV

At least he didn't have to endure the additional torture of the soldiers breaking his legs, which is normally done to those being crucified, to speed up the dying process. He died too quickly for them to do this. I was so glad not to have to witness that additional abuse on him. Oh, the little things that bring gratitude.

All I could do was to stand by the cross, with Jesus on it. He was so helpless, so hurting. It just ripped at my gut, leaving me feeling nauseous.

The angel Gabriel once visited me, or it seemed as though it was a real visit. At this moment, it is hard to imagine there was an angel involved in my life. I'm wondering if I just imagined the visit. After all, what the angel said is very conflicting to me right now: *"Greetings, you who are highly favored! The Lord is with you."*[12] If that were really true, why would God have let this happen? Is this how God treats those who are "highly favored"? Why would God

---

[12] Luke 1:28 NIV

have let any of those terrible things happen to my family, especially today's horrible tragedy, if I were so highly favored?

Today's events just make me miss my husband so much. Joseph was such a good man, a godly man of very high character. Not only did he teach his children about God, but he also taught them about carpentry work. He loved spending time with his children. When Joseph died, I thought I couldn't go on. The pain and heartache were so terrible. I loved him so much. I just ached for months, but I also had children to take care of, and so I did.

This nightmarish day reminds me of a comparable event, the horrible death that Jesus' cousin, John (the Baptist), experienced because of that terrible woman Herodias. His mother Elizabeth and I were pregnant at the same time. John was only a few months older than Jesus. We all grieved John's death, but I had no comprehension of what Elizabeth experienced. Elizabeth had to grieve her son's gruesome death, a death that had no purpose other than the desire of a horrible woman. Oh, a mother should not have to experience the loss of a child. At the time, I couldn't imagine Jesus going through a more horrific experience than the killing of his cousin as a young man. Not only were they family and of the same age, but they were both in similar ministries—loving God and telling others about God. After John was killed, Jesus just wanted to be alone, probably to grieve and pray, and probably because he was just worn out. But the crowds of people wouldn't leave him alone. They were so demanding of his time. I just felt so bad for him. I felt so bad for Elizabeth. I didn't think it could get any worse than John's beheading for feeling lost and beside myself. Oh, I was so wrong.

Absolutely no words can explain this gut-wrenching feeling that I'm experiencing because of my loss of Jesus, my firstborn, the one of whom so much good was said at his birth. The expectations were so high, but now they were snuffed out in just a few hours.

How can I look back at the angel's visit with any understanding other than it was wrong? A mother is not supposed to experience the loss of a child. It's not natural. Was I really "highly favored"? It sure doesn't feel like it.

A huge void has been created within me, and at the same time, I just want to be left alone. I really don't want people around me. It is normal for people to want to provide some sort of comfort, but why do people feel the need to talk with me? I don't want to talk with anyone. There is no energy or desire within me to have a conversation.

Not only is conversation undesirable, but what could possibly be a proper response to some of the things being said? It's only been a few hours since I witnessed my son's gruesome death, and people are saying:

"It will be okay." It won't be okay! My son has just been killed.

"It was meant to be." If it was meant to be, then there is a cruel God out there.

"You'll get over it." How could I ever get over this? I just witnessed first-hand the most horrific abuse that could be inflicted upon my son.

"How are you feeling?" Why do they even have to ask? Isn't it obvious that it's the worst day of my life? Can't they understand that?

"I know how you feel." How could anyone know or even suggest they know how I feel?

Are these people just clueless or rude, or do they just feel they need to say something to satisfy themselves? It really would be best if they just wouldn't talk to me. Maybe sit quietly with me, without talking.

My mind keeps wondering if I did something wrong as a mother. What could I have done differently? How could I have sheltered him from those horrible people? However, as I know Jesus, he was doing and saying what he believed God wanted him to do and say. He was doing God's work. Nothing could have been done or said to convince him otherwise. Nonetheless, it is going to be a nagging thought in my head for a long time to come. What could I have done to have prevented this action?

My Jewish neighbors have been so kind to bring lots of food for my family and me, especially since I didn't have time to prepare the Sabbath meal. That is a really great thing the Jewish community does when there is a death; to bring meals to the family.

One moment the pain is so bad that taking a breath is difficult. The next moment I'm feeling paralyzed—unable to move. This is just the most gut-wrenching experience imaginable. How will I go on trying to live a normal life? I can't even walk around my house without seeing something that reminds me of Jesus.

My mind just goes from shock and disbelief, along with a certain numbness, to racing around with all sorts of thoughts. Over and over, I keep wondering:

Could I have done something to have prevented this horrible event from happening?

Am I being punished for something I have done wrong?

Will I forget the sound of his voice?

Will this empty feeling ever go away? I never knew I could feel so empty. Even with other children around me, I feel completely empty.

Will I be able to show my other children the love they deserve? Will I be able to protect them? I couldn't protect Jesus.

Why couldn't I have died in his place? Oh, how I wish it could have been me instead of Jesus.

The death of a child must be every parent's worst nightmare. No matter how bad you imagine it to be, to experience it is far worse. Even with all the well-meaning people around me, I really need someone who can understand something of what I'm experiencing. Maybe some comfort can come from someone who has experienced something similar? Maybe cousin Elizabeth. I'm going to have to visit her when this all settles down. We celebrated our pregnancies together. Now we have both experienced the unjustifiable killing of our firstborn sons by the most horrible people imaginable. Oh, what a terrible thing for us to have in common.

As some of us are sitting around just feeling numb from the day, there are some seemingly unimportant conversations happening. Some are talking about the darkness that occurred during the last few hours of Jesus being on the cross. I'm not sure it was as noticeable to me as it was to others. It was just such a "dark" time. My eyes weren't even open during much of the time, and when they were, they were full of tears, so why would I notice the darkness? The others are saying the darkness was everywhere, too much for it to have simply been weather-related and too early in the day for it to have been the sun setting. Apparently, the daylight returned. It is all just a blur to me.

The earthquake, which is being discussed, was quite noticeable. It's hard not to notice the earth-shaking, no matter what your emotional condition. We do have periodic earthquakes, but people are saying this one seemed to occur at precisely the same time Jesus died. How coincidental is that? Does it really matter?

What really has me dumbfounded is the stories that are being told regarding the Temple curtain being torn into two pieces, also at the exact same time Jesus died. The sun stopped shining; the earth shook, the Temple curtain was torn into two pieces – what really happened today? It has people talking. It sure seems to be a bit odd, but I really don't have the energy to think about it. I just lost my son, my firstborn. Who really cares about the local news and weather report? I hope to be able just to cry myself to sleep tonight. Maybe this is all just a bad dream.

The Next Day - The Sabbath

I'm totally exhausted. I don't think I slept at all last night. Who could sleep? The sights and sounds of yesterday just kept flashing through my head. When I would start to fall asleep, the same nightmare just ran over and over and over, in my head—just reliving that horrible sight of Jesus on the cross. I'm just numb, and at the same time, my mind keeps racing around in no specific order.

It's the Sabbath. I should go to the synagogue, but I don't want to see anyone. I don't want to talk with anyone. Everyone who sees me will just ask the same question: "How are you doing?" I don't want to tell them. They wouldn't understand if they were told, and it pains me to talk about it. I don't want to see people. I don't want to eat. I just want to curl up in a corner and cry, but there doesn't seem to be any more tears left to come out.

My strength should be coming from God, but I'm not sure about this God thing right now. The psalmist told us in difficult times to *"be still, and know that I am God."*[13] Being still sure didn't get me what I was expecting. How could God let this happen? It was just pure evil that was done to Jesus. There is no other way to describe what was done to him. If God is in control, how could He have let this evil be done, let alone done to someone who had committed his life to tell others about the love of God?

On top of that, what about all that was told to us, all we experienced, all we heard? Was any of it real, or did we just imagine the stories and events?

The angel Gabriel visited me to announce I would be pregnant and would give birth to a son, claiming that *"He will be great and will be called the Son of the Most High. The Lord God will give him the throne of his father David, and he will reign over the house of Jacob forever; his kingdom will never end."*[14] So much for a never-ending kingdom. He's dead! If God really sent that angel,

---

[13] Psalm 46:10 NIV
[14] Luke 1:32-33 NIV

you'd think He would have had a better plan than to let Jesus be killed at only 32 years of age, before he had a chance to be king. Joseph was also told a similar story from an angel that visited him, claiming that *"he will save his people from their sins."*[15] It's rather tough to save people from a tomb!

    Not only that, why did I have to go through the humiliation and ridicule that was experienced during my pregnancy, during the betrothal period? After all, Joseph and I had never had marital relations, so how were we to explain to family and friends my pregnancy? I was scared. They could have stoned me to death, figuring me to be an adulterer. They weren't having any notion of a story so absurd as a claim that the Holy Spirit came upon me, and I became pregnant. Joseph could have sent me away or had me stoned to death, but instead, he took me to be his wife and loved me. I loved him so much. I miss him so much, but I'm also glad he doesn't have to experience this situation. It would have just torn

---

[15] Matthew 1:21 NIV

him apart to have witnessed the events of these last couple of days. Why was I put through that pregnancy experience if Jesus was going to die so early in life?

What about the man called Simeon? When Jesus was eight days old, we took him to be presented in the Temple, to be circumcised, as is the law. While we were there, Simeon held baby Jesus, exclaiming to God, *"for my eyes have seen your salvation."*[16] God's "salvation" was just hung on a cross. What kind of salvation is that?

When Jesus was just a boy of twelve years, he was teaching in the synagogue. No one that young ever teaches in the synagogue. That just doesn't happen. All the people who heard him were amazed at his knowledge. It was clear that God had something special in mind for Jesus. Who could have guessed the "something special" would include being nailed to a cross at the peak of his ministry?

---

[16] Luke 2:30 NIV

When Jesus was baptized, who could have missed the voice coming from heaven saying, *"You are my Son, whom I love, with you I am well pleased."*[17] Doesn't God have a unique way of treating someone He loves!

Surely these types of things are not told to every mother—stories and claims about their sons being saviors and kings. These statements were so special to me; I cherished each one as if they were each a gift. How quickly those gifts were destroyed! At the time, it seemed like there was a big plan in place. Who could have imagined all that preparation and planning was to end on a cross? How good was that planning? If this was part of some master plan, something sure seems to be wrong with the plan.

Apparently, there were people who weren't pleased with Jesus, especially the Pharisees, but why? He was constantly doing good for people. He loved people, even people who were not loved by others. He did so much good for people.

---

[17] Mark 1:11 NIV

Jesus was special, way beyond what most people knew. That's why I had him solve the problem at the wedding in Cana. The problem of running out of wine is a terrible problem for a bridegroom, so I mentioned it to Jesus. He told me that it wasn't time for him to start doing miracles yet. That may have been so, but, nonetheless, the water in the jars turned into wine. Not just any wine, the best wine! Should I have listened to him instead of pushing him to perform some miracle before he was ready? Maybe I pushed him too fast into his ministry. Maybe he wasn't ready to begin, and that's why he wasn't received well by everyone.

Jesus' disciples constantly told so many stories of the healings he performed. Everyone he healed must have known how special he was. The people who were healed would run through the streets proclaiming what Jesus had done for them. He healed people of leprosy, of being crippled, of dropsy, of being blind, deaf, and dumb, of fevers. How could this not be seen by everyone as miraculous and amazingly awesome?

The disciples tell me that when the soldiers came to arrest Jesus at the Mount of Olives, Peter cut off the right ear of Malchus, the high priest's servant. Most people would have agreed the disciples were within their rights to put up a fight. Not Jesus. He took the time to put the ear back on Malchus. He healed a man who was unjustifiably arresting him. Even in such a dire situation, Jesus thought about someone other than himself.

There is no misunderstanding. Jesus healed people! He healed people by touching them. Some were healed by touching his garments. Others were healed just because he spoke a healing word from quite a distance away. He healed people!

Jesus was an awesome teacher. Large crowds of people would come to hear his teaching and preaching of the good news of the kingdom of God. It was obvious from his teaching encounter in the synagogue when he was 12 years old that he was a gifted teacher. He also had an interesting way of teaching by using parables. They weren't always easy to understand, but they were insightful. He also gave wonderful sermons. The most popular one is referred to as the Sermon on the Mount. Such truths he exclaimed that day. Whenever he taught, the people were amazed. His teaching was unlike anything they had ever heard.

His ability to cast demons from people may have been more miraculous than the physical healings. In effect, it too was a healing—a spiritual healing. When the crowds would watch, they were just amazed. These healings demonstrated Jesus had authority over the evil spirits, and what a blessing it was to those who had been possessed for years.

So, healing people and casting out demons was amazing, but what about the people who were raised from the dead? That is just unheard of, at least anywhere I have ever been. There are multiple stories of Jesus bringing people back to life from the dead, but when he gave the command for his friend Lazarus to come out of the grave, everyone was speechless. Mary and Martha were beside themselves. After all, Lazarus had been dead for several days.

From my perspective, after hearing him teach, he clearly taught a message of love, but he didn't love just the religious leaders or the wealthy citizens. No, he taught people to invite the poor, the disabled, and the lame to banquets. He loved babies and little children, welcoming them even when others tried to make them go away. He loved everyone, and he taught us that we are to love as he loved. Not many people can follow in his footsteps.

In addition to love, he spent a lot of time teaching about forgiveness, which was another topic that was near and dear to his heart. Jesus was great at forgiving people. Even as a child, I remember him being willing to forgive someone who did something against him. He emphasized the importance of forgiving others so that God will forgive us.

He never asked for money for any of the things he did. There was no personal gain for the work he performed. He just wanted everyone to hear about God, to repent, and put their trust in God.

He was willing to socialize with everyone, even tax collectors and sinners. When he was questioned about this, he responded by saying, *"It is not the healthy who need a doctor, but the sick. I have not come to call the righteous, but sinners to repentance."*[18] He loved everyone.

How could any person have wanted to kill him? He taught of love and forgiveness. He healed people. He fed people. The people loved him. He did nothing to harm them. Why did they turn on him and kill him?

Peter just told me that after Jesus was arrested, he was taken to the Sanhedrin (the court of rabbis) for them to hear the case against him. Peter said they could find no evidence against Jesus, but then someone stood up, made a false claim, and before you knew it, the crowd was shouting crucify him—going from nothing wrong to crucify him within minutes. How could God have let this happen? It was His rabbis who made this happen.

---

[18] Luke 5:31-32 NIV

I just can't stop thinking about him—about what he was like and the things he did. Is he really gone—never to be seen or heard from again? I have so many memories.

Jesus loved to sing, especially songs of praise to God. Some of his disciples mentioned how he led them in a hymn after they finished eating the other evening, the evening he was arrested. Singing is such an awesome way of praising God, and Jesus loved to praise God.

Such a man of God he was. I have never known anyone who spent as much time praying to God. It was obvious that he loved God beyond anything else. One day while he was teaching, someone asked him what the greatest commandment was. Without hesitation, he responded, *"Love the Lord your God with all your heart and with all your soul and with all your strength and with all your mind."*[19] There was no doubt in his mind that God was absolutely the most important thing—nothing else was even close.

---

[19] Luke 10:27 NIV

He was also so compassionate! He seemed to have a special sense for people who were harassed and helpless. It was as if he knew they were hurting when no one else knew it.

On one of his journeys, according to Matthew, Jesus had such compassion on the people that he instructed his disciples to pray, asking, *"the Lord of the harvest, therefore, to send out workers into his harvest field."*[20] He wanted God to send more helpers for these people. Not just to help meet their physical needs, but he also wanted everyone to hear God's good news.

Then there is the story told by Luke about the widow who had lost her son. Some people were carrying his body out of town for burial. Jesus just looked at her and had such compassion for her that he simply told the young man to get up. How shocked everyone must have been when the young man sat up and started talking. No one asked Jesus to perform a miracle or any such thing. His heart must have just broken for that woman.

---

[20] Matthew 9:38 NIV

There are two stories told by Mark of Jesus feeding large groups of people, at least 5,000 people one of the times and 4,000 the other. Apparently, one of the times Jesus felt bad for the large crowd of people that had been following him, as he said, *"I have compassion for these people; they have already been with me three days and have nothing to eat. If I send them home hungry, they will collapse on the way, because some of them have come a long distance."*[21] He could have easily stopped teaching and told the people to go and find food. No one would have thought any less of him, but he didn't do that. He instructed his disciples to feed the people. Such compassion he had for people.

I don't remember the last time I told him that I loved him or that I was proud of him. I don't think I ever showed my appreciation enough to him. To be honest, I don't think any of our friends or family appreciated or understood Jesus. That must have been what he spoke of that Sabbath when he was teaching in the synagogue

---

[21] Mark 8:2-3 NIV

and stated: *"A prophet is not without honor except in his own town, among his relatives and in his own home."*[22] This really upset the people who were present, but now that I think about it, we really didn't give him the respect he deserved. From what I've heard from his disciples, everywhere else he taught, they praised his teaching. I could have been more encouraging to him.

My mind is racing in so many directions, so many questions. I'm crying one minute, reminiscing the next, while angry the next moment. How am I going to survive?

Why did he go to Jerusalem that day? Apparently, he told others he was about to be killed. Somehow, he knew it was going to happen. It is beside me how he knew, but nonetheless, why did he go there if he knew he was going to be killed? Couldn't he have gone somewhere else where they wanted to hear his teaching, where they really loved him? There's a story going around that he didn't even try to defend himself when he was with the Sanhedrin.

---

[22] Mark 6:4 NIV

He just remained quiet during much of the interrogation. Why did he do that? Surely, he could have explained what he was teaching and what he believed. They would have understood. As I think about it, I'm angry with Jesus. If he didn't care about himself, couldn't he have known what this would do to others, such as me? He had such compassion for non-relatives. Why couldn't he have shown some of that compassion to his own mother by talking with the rabbis so they wouldn't have killed him? Oh, I can't believe I'm blaming Jesus.

My mind is just racing around with all sorts of thoughts and in a fog at the same time.

Tomorrow, we are to take spices to the tomb to prepare Jesus' body. How can I even think of what to take? What to take to the tomb of my son?

Chapter 3: The Resurrection

The First Day of the Week

Typically, the body of a deceased person is anointed with spices and prepared for burial the day after death occurs. As yesterday was the Sabbath, we were not permitted to perform this activity for Jesus. We had to wait until today, which is considered to be the third day. I know it is important for us to go to the tomb and finalize the preparation of his body today. I'm just not sure I can do it. I can't imagine going there and seeing him—his cold, lifeless body. I'm just numb thinking about it. I can't eat. I can't sleep. I can't think straight.

The other women are saying they are going, so I'll go, simply because he is my son, but I feel sick. I can't imagine doing anything. I don't even think I have the strength to walk to the tomb, but I'll try.

While walking to the tomb, it is very quiet. None of us are in the mood for talking. We are all still in disbelief. Out of nowhere, one of the ladies asks how we are going to be able to move the stone that is in front of the tomb. The stone is very large and heavy. We have also heard that Pilate ordered for the tomb to be made extra secure by placing a seal on the stone and having a guard posted outside the tomb. Will the guard allow us to attend to Jesus' body? Will the guard help us move the stone? With Pilate's seal on the stone, the guard may not be permitted to allow the stone to be moved, even for the mother of Jesus.

There is extra security because there is concern that someone will try to steal Jesus' body. Why? Why would someone want to steal Jesus' body? Why does Pilate care if someone steals Jesus' body? He didn't care about Jesus when Jesus was alive; why would he care when Jesus is dead?

At the Tomb

We meet as early as possible to make certain we have plenty of time for the burial preparations, but apparently, we are not walking fast enough for Mary Magdalene. She seems to have more energy than the rest of us as she is running towards the tomb. Running is not something I will be doing today. I barely have enough strength to walk.

We see off in the distance that Mary Magdalene must have arrived at the tomb because she comes to a stop, a rather sudden stop. We can't tell what she sees.

Upon arriving at the tomb, we can now see what Mary was looking at because the stone had been rolled from the entrance. When we look inside the tomb, there is no body. Jesus' body is gone. The only things remaining are a pile of strips of linen and a neatly folded burial cloth. My first thoughts are what have they done with Jesus' body, and why did they remove the linen from his body? Who did this? They tortured and bullied an innocent man, and then they killed him in the most horrific means imaginable. Now they don't even have the decency to leave his dead body alone.

I notice that someone is nearby and go to ask him what's been done with Jesus' body. I don't know who he is, but he is dressed in extremely bright, white clothes. It sure doesn't seem normal for someone to be dressed in white clothes in and around the tombs, and these clothes are even whiter than anything I have ever seen. As I approach, he says, *"Do not be afraid, for I know that you are looking for Jesus, who was crucified. He is not here; he has risen, just as he said."*[23]

RISEN! How can that be? Who is telling us this news? What sort of a nasty trick is this? Can it be true? I don't know if I am more afraid, scared, happy, or just full of confusion. It is too unbelievable. We must tell the disciples. I have the energy to run now. We must

---

[23] Matthew 28:5-6 NIV

find Jesus' disciples. They need to know what we've seen and what we've been told.

We reach the disciples, but no one wants to believe us. They think we are crazy. I'm even questioning what I am saying. After all, doesn't everyone imagine their deceased loved one is still alive, not dead? For whatever reason, Peter decided he must see for himself. So, he takes off running, along with another of the disciples. I am trying to keep up with them, but they are running much too fast for me. When I arrive at the tomb, they are just staring at the empty tomb, at the strips of linen, wondering, "Where is Jesus' body?"

The disciples are in disbelief about Jesus rising from the dead—it just doesn't happen, but where is Jesus' body? However, with no sign of Jesus, the disciples and the rest of us have decided to return to our homes—all of us except Mary Magdalene. Mary is just sobbing while standing outside the tomb. There's no convincing her to leave, so we have decided to go without her. She'll return when she's ready.

We've only been home a short while, and I can hear Mary Magdalene calling joyfully while running towards us. She is absolutely totally different from how we left her at the tomb. She is full of joy and excitement, but she is so excited and breathing so fast from running that it is hard to understand her. It is obvious she experienced something that excited her. I may regret having left the tomb.

Mary finally calms down enough to tell us what happened. She is telling how, while she was at the tomb crying, a person she thought was the gardener approached her and said her name. As soon as she heard his voice, she knew it was Jesus, alive and in the flesh! Is it truly possible?

There is no doubt Mary Magdalene had an experience that totally changed her demeanor, but could it really have been Jesus? No one ever comes out of the tombs – alive! The Roman soldiers make certain of that. The Roman soldiers have refined the method of killing by crucifixion. Not only was Jesus nearly dead when they nailed him to the cross because of the crown of thorns and beatings and floggings, but there were also the horrific things that happened to his body as he hung there. He was clearly dead! Then, after everyone knew he was dead, a soldier pierced Jesus' side just to confirm he was dead. It's been said the soldiers watch for both blood and water to flow, which somehow confirms death. I don't understand it, but I watched them do it. They knew he was dead. There's no doubt about it. It was their job to know. Then, after all that, he was placed in a cold, dark tomb where he had no medication, or food, or drink. If there was any life remaining in him, which wasn't possible, how could he have moved that huge stone in such a weakened condition? It's just not possible for Jesus to be alive—how could he be? But Mary wouldn't make up such a story. What am I to believe?

It's more likely the soldiers, or the temple leaders, are trying to make a mockery of Jesus and his followers. What other explanation could there be?

Whatever is happening, I sure didn't consider any of it when this day started. It's not even noontime. What is the rest of the day going to include?

Reflection

As the day progresses, others claim to have seen him. How can I let myself believe it? To allow such hope and then to have my spirit crushed again would be just too painful, but of course, I want to believe it.

There is talk about Jesus having had the power to raise people from the dead as he did with his friend Lazarus, and the daughter of Jairus, and the widow's son, but who could have raised Jesus? There's no one else with that sort of power. Who could have done it?

I surely want to believe. Do I dare allow myself to have the hope he is alive? If I do, I must believe this is all part of God's plan, a plan that is not possible for me to comprehend. Forty-eight hours ago, I was so devastated I could not think—I could hardly breathe—the unthinkable was happening—my son was being crucified. Now, I sit here with the hope that he is alive. Should I have believed more throughout Jesus' life, starting with my pregnancy? Was God communicating with me all along, and I just wasn't paying attention? Oh, the stories that I'm now remembering. Not just remembering, but I'm thinking about the past events totally differently than I did over the last couple of days.

    I was pledged to be married to Joseph – a wonderful, godly man. Then I get the announcement from an angel that I'm pregnant. I had never been with a man—how could it be true? I'll never forget those words from the angel: *"Greetings, you who are highly favored! The Lord is with you."*[24] I must admit I was frightened as well. According to the law, I could have been killed, along with my unborn baby. It was so fortunate for me that Joseph

---

[24] Luke 1:28 NIV

also had a visit from an angel, which confirmed the origin of my pregnancy. That turn of events should have been more than enough for me to remember throughout my life that God was at work, at work for something big. Unfortunately, the busyness of life seems to have clouded my thoughts and memories of God working in my life.

How could I ever forget the greeting I received during my pregnancy when I visited my cousin Elizabeth? She was also pregnant at the same time, slightly further along in her pregnancy than I was. Elizabeth claimed that *"as soon as the sound of your greeting reached my ears, the baby in my womb leaped for joy."*[25] I don't know that I fully appreciated what Elizabeth was saying that day, especially when she said that I was blessed. I do remember just spontaneously breaking out into a song of praise to God. I wish I had maintained that constant attitude of praise throughout the rest of my life.

---

[25] Luke 1:44 NIV

A Mother's Perspective: From Joy to Anguish and Back Again   by Kevin Stine

I don't know if anyone else remembers the trip that Joseph took me on while I was pregnant with Jesus, a trip that included riding on a donkey. I wasn't just pregnant; I was nearly ready to give birth. It's hard for me to remember exactly, but I seem to remember riding that donkey for something like every day for a week or more. I would not recommend such a trip to anyone who is pregnant. What was I thinking when I agreed to accompany Joseph on that trip?

As I reflect over Jesus' life, there really is so much to be told, so much that is unbelievable unless you were there. It truly is not possible to forget the night Jesus was born—in a stable. Who could have planned it any better? After riding on the donkey for a week, we got to sleep in the stable, and my baby was born in the presence of the animals. Then we were visited by a group of shepherds, men who had a story to tell of a visit they had from an angel. They claimed the angel referred to our baby as the Christ, the Messiah. That is so similar to what the first angel said to Joseph. I just treasured the things these men said, but I must admit it is confusing to me how Jesus can save people if he is crucified—dead. Is it possible he is alive and ready to bring salvation to his people?

When Jesus was younger, we were constantly amazed at what happened or what was said on his behalf. We knew there was something extra special about him, but we were still repeatedly blown away by these things. There are so many stories.

When the time of my purification was over, we took Jesus to the temple to have him consecrated to God, as was the Law of Moses. While there, we were approached by a man called Simeon. I believe he was a priest, but we were not sure. He said some amazing things, including, *"This child is destined to cause the falling and rising of many in Israel, and to be a sign that will be spoken against, so that the thoughts of many hearts will be revealed. And a sword will pierce your own soul too."*[26] I remember wondering about these strange words being said to the parents of a newborn baby. Jesus was only days old, and this man was prophesying about

---

[26] Luke 2:34-35 NIV

his future; he was basically saying Jesus would be a rebel. That was a bit overwhelming for new parents to comprehend. And then, he also seemed to be foretelling about me. Could he have been talking about the pain I endured when they hung Jesus on the cross, literally when they pierced him with that spear? How could Simeon have known? Was he a prophet?

How could I ever forget the visit of the Magi, the wise men from the east? Oh, that caravan of men and camels was so large. I had never previously witnessed such a procession. They claimed they were following a special star that appeared in the sky, which was leading them to see the new ruler, the king who was born in Bethlehem, as was written about by the prophets. They claimed Jesus was that newly born king. We had no idea what to think regarding these statements. And then, the gifts they brought—gold, frankincense, and myrrh. No one that I ever knew had received such gifts. After talking with others, we learned these were common gifts to be given to a king. These Magi truly believed they were visiting a king. Little did they know he would be killed on a cross, before any opportunity of being a king, before being a ruler of any sort. Unless, of course, he is alive!

Not many people know about the angelic visits that both Joseph and I received announcing my pregnancy. We didn't tell many people because we didn't think many would believe such a story. We really didn't think anyone would believe us if we told them there were more angelic visits. When Jesus was very young, Joseph received an angelic visit in a dream. The angel said we needed to take Jesus to Egypt to protect him, as Herod was searching for Jesus in order to have him killed. The fear that overcame me when Joseph told me about this dream was beyond imagination. Joseph instantly believed what he was told and immediately started preparing to take his family to Egypt in the middle of the night. I'm not sure how much help I was. I just couldn't stop thinking about someone trying to kill my baby. Why would Herod want to kill my baby? He had never even met any of us. I then wondered if this could possibly be what Simeon was talking about when he said a sword would pierce my soul as well.

Was he saying Herod would kill my baby and me? I was so concerned and scared as we set out for our journey to Egypt, in the dark of the night; that very night—no time to plan, no time to say goodbyes to friends or family. We just got up and left according to what we were told to do.

After living in Egypt a while, Joseph had another angelic visit, in a dream. This time he was told Herod had died and we could all return to Israel. Meanwhile, we learned that Herod had all baby boys killed, any baby boys that would have been about the same age as Jesus. I couldn't imagine what those families experienced. We were to return, with our little boy being perfectly alive. My mind raced with thoughts and questions such as, will they notice Jesus is the only boy of that age? Will they know their babies were killed because Herod was trying to kill Jesus? How will they treat Jesus? My concern was now for Jesus, not that he would be killed but for how he would be treated by others, especially those that lost a little boy of the same age. What a horrific ordeal those families went through, all because Herod wanted to kill Jesus.

Every year, along with a large gathering of friends and relatives, we would make the trip to Jerusalem for the Feast of the Passover. When Jesus was twelve years old, just like every previous year, we made the trip. When the Feast was over, all the families packed up and headed home. After we had been traveling for a day or so, we noticed Jesus wasn't with us. It may seem strange to believe we didn't know the whereabouts of our son, but it was very common for all the children to travel together—not necessarily in the company of their parents. We had traveled to other places similarly, and Jesus was always close by; he was always near us. However, this time he was not in the group, and no one knew where he was. I started to panic. Even if we could assume that he was left behind in Jerusalem, he had already been alone for at least a day and a night, and we would be another full day returning. All I could think about were such thoughts as had he been abducted? Was he hurt? Where would he sleep? What would he eat? We traveled as quickly as we could, but there was not much chance at making the donkey travel as fast as I wanted to go. As soon as we got back to Jerusalem, we started asking everyone if they had seen Jesus. Finally, after being separated from him for a total of three days, we found him in the temple courts. What a safe place for him to be, but much to our surprise, he wasn't just treated as a lost boy. He was listening and asking questions of the elders, but he was also answering questions. He simply amazed those in his presence. Much to my dismay, it didn't even seem like he missed us at all. He really seemed like he was "in his element." He seemed to be surprised we had been searching for him. In fact, his response went something like: *"Didn't you know I had to be in my Father's house?"*[27] It really didn't make complete sense to us at the time, but I think I'm starting to get a better idea as to what he meant.

Throughout his childhood development, it was very clear Jesus was unlike any other child. His wisdom and maturity developed much faster than all the other children. Then, as an adult, there were countless stories telling of his wonderful actions.

---

[27] Luke 2:49 NIV

What an amazingly wonderful man of God he had become. I wasn't always present with him, but thanks to his disciples, stories got back to me. It was evident in all he did that he loved God and that God was with him.

When Jesus was ready to be baptized, he went to his cousin John. As Jesus came out of the water, the disciples said they heard a heavenly voice saying that God was pleased with Jesus. It wasn't just another adult talking; it was Yahweh, the God of all creation, who was pleased with my son. When I heard this story, I was so proud. What more could a mother desire!

Immediately after his baptism, Jesus went into the desert. I did not know why, and to say I was a bit concerned is an understatement. He went into the desert without any food or water. How could he survive? He was there for 40 days. We could not imagine what was going on during that time. There was no way for us even to know if he was alive. After Jesus returned from the desert, we were told he was tempted by the devil during those 40 days, and he had nothing to eat or drink during the entire time—an absolute fast. How was that possible? Why would he voluntarily place himself in that situation? He obviously survived, but we have no idea how. We understand he held off the devil's temptations by quoting words from the Torah. I am so glad he learned the teachings of Moses and could apply them, but I'm still confused why he went into the desert in the first place. Was he following some directive from God?

There are endless stories his disciples would tell every time they would return home from their travels with Jesus—stories about Jesus, things he did, and how he responded to situations. It must have been so exciting traveling around with Jesus—never a dull moment.

One of my favorite stories they would tell is about a time Jesus and his disciples were in a boat crossing the lake. I believe they said it was the Sea of Galilee. Jesus was so sound asleep when a storm came upon them that he did not even wake up. He just continued sleeping as a baby sleeps in a cradle that is gently rocked, but there was no gentle rocking of this boat. Jesus had spent very little time on boats, let alone on a boat in a storm. It's amazing he could sleep. I think he could sleep through anything. When the disciples woke him, he simply spoke, and the wind and waves calmed down completely. The wind and waves obeyed him. The storm did not seem to faze Jesus at all, but the real point is that the wind and waves obeyed him!

It's always been known there are demon-possessed people, but I never knew anyone who could successfully cast demons out of people. Among the many strengths Jesus had, this was one of them. He was successful at calling the demons out of many people, just by his words. One of the most unique displays of this came when he was in the Gerasenes region. The story goes that the demons begged Jesus to cast them into a herd of pigs that was near them. Jesus agreed. The demons immediately went into the pigs, and the herd subsequently ran into the lake and drowned—all of them. Jesus spoke, and the demons responded!

Something else Jesus did amazingly well was the healing of people. There were times he just spoke a word, and the person was healed. Sometimes the person was close by, and other times they were a long way off. It didn't seem to matter. Jesus just had to speak, and the people were healed. However, from the stories told to me, Jesus also had some other very unusual ways of healing people. Those are the stories I remember the most. I never did know why, but there were numerous occasions in which Jesus used his own spit in the healing process. Apparently, one time he put his fingers into the ears of a deaf and dumb man, then he spat, touched the man's tongue, said some words, and the man could hear and speak. Not a normal routine for a physician, but then a physician never made a deaf man hear. Apparently, there was another time in which Jesus spat on a blind man's eyes, and the man could then see. And yet another time, Jesus made some mud with his spit, placed the mud on the man's eyes, told him to wash, and after washing, the man could see. What was it with Jesus' spit? It worked, but it was definitely a unique technique to use for healing.

Something that always stood out to me was the way Jesus would disarm a potentially hostile situation by remaining calm and saying very few words. A great example of this is the time some Pharisees brought a woman to Jesus, a woman who was accused of being an adulterer. I wonder if this story stands out to me because I could almost relate to this woman. She was accused of committing adultery. When I was pregnant with Jesus, there was a fear in me that I would be accused of the same. I wasn't, but no one else knew how I became pregnant. I could have been stoned to death, just as these accusers were ready to stone her to death, as is the law for such an action. Part of the story includes the Pharisees trying somehow to trap Jesus regarding his response to this situation. They were trying to bring harm to him somehow, and at the same time, creating a crowd mentality bent on stoning this woman. Apparently, without getting upset or angry at them, Jesus simply said, *"Let any one of you who is without sin be the first to throw a stone at her."*[28] That's all he said. Not some long, drawn-out speech.

---

[28] John 8:7 NIV

From that simple statement, the accusatory crowd started to disperse until there was no one remaining except the woman and Jesus. Such a gift he had for remaining calm in potentially stressful situations.

How can I also not reminisce over Jesus' years in our family, especially his older years? I hope I don't forget the wonderful stories of Jesus and our family, the good and the not-so-good.

As he grew into a young man, Joseph taught him much about the building trades. After all, that is what Joseph did to support our family, as that is what his father did to support their family. As Jesus was the eldest child, he was the first to be taught by his father. When Joseph died, Jesus continued working in the building trades to continue supporting our family. After Jesus started in the ministry, his brothers continued to work in the family business, continuing to support all of us.

I don't know that our family was much different from any other family. We had our difficult moments. Some would just refer to it as sibling rivalries, but I think there was a bit of jealousy as well on the part of my other children. It was very clear to everyone that Jesus was different. His knowledge, his wisdom, his basic demeanor all showed him to be different than others. There was a day that Jesus' siblings must have reached a boiling point regarding their attitude towards their older brother. When Jesus was at the home of our neighbor, his siblings interrupted the visit rather harshly by basically claiming that he was crazy. It was rather apparent they wanted him to stop with this ministry stuff and to just work in the carpentry shop. It also had to be quite clear to Jesus that his siblings did not think very highly of him. In fact, many local people were in this same category. I'm sure that is why Jesus once claimed that he did not receive any honor or respect at home. He was correct. He did not receive encouragement, or praise, or honor. His family really had no idea who he was. Even though I was told numerous times during Jesus' early days, I think the busyness of life would get in the way of me remembering the specialties of Jesus. I never told anyone, beyond Joseph, what had been told to me by an angel or what Simeon had said. Who would have believed me? I'm sure it would have caused additional strife between my other children and Jesus.

As I sit here reminiscing over Jesus' life, the alleged sightings of him continue to be reported. There is so much I don't understand, but why would these people make up such stories? In fact, if the stories aren't true, the storytellers could get into very serious trouble with the authorities. I really have no choice other than to believe that Jesus is alive! That he has risen from the dead! It's not that the tomb is empty because Jesus' body was moved. It's empty because Jesus walked out of it! Such unexplainable joy for a mother, unlike anything imaginable. To go from the depths of grief and anguish, gut-wrenching anguish, to extreme joy, in less than forty-eight hours is more than I could have imagined. It may be hard to believe, but I'm once again having difficulty breathing while tears stream down my face. It appears as if my body doesn't know how to respond to such intense joy—such a myriad of emotions. It's as if I'm being choked—so many emotions in such a short time. God has to be at work throughout this entire situation. There is no other possible explanation.

Stories of Jesus Sightings

There is so much commotion all around us. A lot is happening quickly. It has only been a few hours since we first arrived at the tomb, but by now, I doubt there is anyone in Jerusalem that hasn't heard the news. Such a story travels like a wildfire around this place. To think that early this morning, I wasn't even sure I wanted to go to the tomb, and now the potential outcome of this day is just beyond words, beyond anyone's wildest imagination.

It was amazing to hear about the sightings of Jesus. The mere hearing of them brings extreme joy to me. Any mother would be joyful when her child does something amazing, but this is so far beyond anything imaginable. To describe it as being joyful seems to be a very inadequate statement.

As the stories of "Jesus sightings" grow in numbers, the authorities seem to be doing everything possible to refute the stories. They can't tolerate or accept the truth that Jesus has risen from the dead, that nothing they could do could keep him in the grave, even after following Pilate's orders for extra security. By the way, the guards were highly trained, and they could be killed for failing their assignment, for allowing Jesus' body to be removed. None of us women or Jesus' disciples would have been able to overpower the guards to take Jesus' body. And since the chief priests couldn't keep him in the grave, they have made up a story saying his body was stolen. Surely, they didn't think through the reality of someone being able to steal a dead body from a guarded tomb, from a tomb guarded by elite Roman soldiers.

Some are saying he was never truly dead, and as such, he really didn't come back to life. Didn't they see his body before it was placed into the tomb? Didn't they witness the torture Jesus experienced before being hung on the cross? Then he hung on the cross and experienced even more unimaginable torture, pain, and suffering. He was dead! But just to be certain, the soldier pierced Jesus' side with a sword. There is really no way that Jesus lived through all of that. The soldiers knew he was dead. Everyone knew he was dead, but if there had been even the slightest bit of life left in him when he was placed in the tomb, his body would have had to heal itself in that cold, dark, damp tomb, with no healing salves or medicines. That is an environment for infections to develop, not healing to occur. And then, after all that, without having food or water for days, he would have had to gain enough strength to roll the stone away, all by himself, a nearly impossible feat for a completely healthy man. Oh, and then, after moving the stone, he would have had to get past the guards. How could any sane person truly believe that Jesus was not dead when he was placed in the tomb, and on top of that, to believe that he healed enough to let himself out of the grave?

No, Jesus' body was not stolen, and yes, Jesus did die. The fact is that Jesus is once again alive. He rose from the dead. God sent His angels to move the stone, to free Jesus from the grave. This whole situation reminds me of the words spoken by the angel Gabriel when he visited me: *"For nothing will be impossible with*

God."[29] He can cause a virgin to give birth to His Son, and He can raise the dead—especially His Son!

It's just the first day of the week, the day we learned the tomb was empty, and Jesus has made several appearances. Even though I haven't seen him yet, it gets me so excited to think about each sighting as told about by others.

As Mary Magdalene was leaving the tomb to go tell his disciples what the angel had said to her, Jesus suddenly appeared and said, *"Do not be afraid. Go and tell my brothers to go to Galilee; there, they will see me."*[30] She was so excited. I wonder if her feet even touched the ground as she ran to tell the disciples. There is no doubt she saw and talked with Jesus.

Two of Jesus' followers were walking along the road to Emmaus when they had an encounter with Jesus. They did not recognize him at first. He explained to them how Christ, the

---

[29] Luke 1:37 New American Standard Bible (NASB)
[30] Matthew 28:10 NIV

Messiah, had to suffer, according to what the prophets had said. After eating with them, they recognized him, and then he disappeared. To say that I'm still a little confused is an understatement. How could they not recognize him one moment and then recognize him the next? Will I be able to recognize my own son?

The two that encountered Jesus along the road to Emmaus went to the other disciples to tell them about their experience. While they were still telling their story, Jesus appeared to them all. Jesus showed them his hands and feet. He ate with them. He told how this all had to happen to fulfill the Scriptures: *"The Messiah will suffer and rise from the dead on the third day."*[31] All this was needed so that repentance and forgiveness of sins could be preached. He also told them that God would be sending His Holy Spirit. I'm not sure that any of us truly understand what is meant by the Holy Spirit. We should be finding out soon.

---

[31] Luke 24:46 NIV

As the days progress into weeks, the sightings of Jesus continue. There should be no doubt in anyone's mind that he is alive. There's no way that all these people would be telling these stories about seeing Jesus if the stories weren't true.

Thomas had not seen Jesus in those initial encounters. However, a week later, when Thomas was with the other disciples, Jesus came into their presence, even though the doors were locked. He just appeared out of nowhere, which caught everyone by surprise, but it was what Thomas needed exactly. It took Thomas placing his fingers into Jesus' hands before he would believe that Jesus was alive. He now believes!

Another story regarding a sighting of Jesus seems to involve Jesus cooking breakfast for many of his disciples. Apparently, a group of them had gone out fishing one morning, and as it sometimes goes, they weren't catching any fish. A man on shore called to them and suggested they cast their net on the right side of the boat. When they did this, they caught so many fish in the net they couldn't haul the net onto the boat. At that point, John told Peter that the man was Jesus. Peter, being a spontaneous person, jumped into the water and swam toward Jesus. Why he couldn't just ride the boat in with the rest doesn't make sense to me, but that is just the way Peter functions—spontaneously! Jesus had a fire going and offered to cook some fish for them. Jesus always had that loving, servant attitude toward others. Just a few days ago, he was crucified on a cross, buried, then rose from the dead—probably one of the biggest miracles of all time—and now he just prepares a casual meal for his friends. There's no one else like him. I believe this was at least the third time Jesus appeared to his disciples after his resurrection.

Following Jesus' resurrection from the dead, his mere presence presented all the proof needed that he was alive. Besides the encounters with his disciples, he has appeared to a single group of more than 500 people, speaking to them about the kingdom of God. Imagine that—over 500 people who are witnesses of his resurrection, people not listed as his closest friends. These people have no reason to pass along a fictitious story. They would have no benefit to gain from such a story. How could anyone argue that Jesus has not risen?

For me, the most amazing encounter since his resurrection has been between Jesus and his brother James. There's often conflict between brothers in a family, I understand that, but it still breaks a mother's heart to see any of her children not getting along, especially once they've entered their adult years. James has had no respect for Jesus or Jesus' ministry. He was likely the most outspoken sibling against Jesus. I think he took the lead in getting the other brothers to tell Jesus to leave home and not return. But something has happened following Jesus' crucifixion and resurrection. James has had a complete transformation, not just in his relationship with Jesus but also in his overall life. He has quickly become a different person. In such a short amount of time, he has gone from speaking against Jesus to becoming a spokesperson on Jesus' behalf. There's no more jealousy or bitterness. He's even talking about possibly writing a book about being a follower of

Jesus. Not only that, he's talking with the other siblings, not to turn them against Jesus, but rather to convince them that they have been wrong about Jesus. And not just James—it seems as if Jude is also now understanding of their brother. Understanding and wanting to follow him! What could make a mother happier!

Chapter 4: The Ascension

I have just learned that Jesus has been taken up into heaven. There was no death. No pain. No suffering. Apparently, he was talking with his disciples and blessing them one moment, and the next, he was gone—just vanishing into the clouds.

Forty days is way too short of a time to have had Jesus back in my life, but to have had him back at all is nothing short of a miracle. The excruciating pain I encountered when he was taken from me at the cross had to have been the worst imaginable. The news that he has ascended into heaven has left me feeling no pain or heartache. I must admit there is a bit of sorrow because a mother wants her children to be around forever, but this is so very different. We know he is going to be with God, his Father. Will he be missed? Of course, he will be missed! However, he has also promised that he is preparing a place for us and he will return for us. What a joyous day that will be! We can now look forward to that day, a hope we did not have when he was taken from us on Calvary.

Is it possible for anyone to experience the amazing joy that has come to me? Can a mother experience any greater joy than on the day she gives birth to her child? No matter how many children she has, there is still joy at their births. In contrast, there cannot be any greater despair than the death of a child. I think I have experienced the ultimate joy because I first experienced the greatest despair. If that is true, then we surely can assume that, in order to experience joy in our lives, we will also have to experience some despair, some hardships, and heartaches.

As we have experienced this amazing joy in our lives, some of the disciples and us women have decided to meet daily for prayer and encouragement while waiting for the Holy Spirit to come, as was promised by Jesus. We are all seeing things from a different perspective now. During this time together, I know we will receive encouragement by reminding each other about the things Jesus taught, as well as our thoughts, feelings, and experiences we had with Jesus.

Marriage

As the women and I meet together, along with the disciples, I'm reminded of the many times Jesus made comparisons to a Jewish wedding, often referring to himself as the bridegroom and his followers as the bride. Even though I am very familiar with Jewish wedding customs, the comparisons were not always easy for me to understand. However, as I look back at my marriage and think about the marriage process, a lot is starting to make sense.

In most circumstances, the father of the bridegroom chooses the bride for his son, as Joseph's father did by choosing me to be Joseph's bride. This is what I'm also starting to understand about our God, Jehovah. He chooses or invites those who will be the followers, the bride, of His Son, Jesus. According to the prophet Zephaniah, *"He has consecrated those he has invited."*[32] God has

---

[32] Zephaniah 1:7 NIV

consecrated us, set us apart from all the rest, to be the Bride of Christ.

Then the bridegroom must pay the Mohar, the bride-price. After I was chosen by Joseph's father, Joseph paid the agreed-upon bride-price. Similarly, Jesus paid the bride-price for his bride, his followers, by forgiving each of us our sins, by dying on the cross. No greater gift could have been given to his bride.

I am certain that my father looked out for my best interest when he and Joseph's father discussed our potential marriage, but prior to them signing the Ketubbah, the contract, I was given a chance to give my consent or not. This also makes me think back on what we were taught about Rebecca and how she must have been totally shocked when Abraham's servant came seeking her to marry Isaac. Rebecca was asked if she wanted to go or not. She consented to go. Likewise, those who have been invited to follow Jesus are given that same opportunity to say yes or no, regarding following him.

The Ketubbah is a legal document the bridegroom must also sign. Once Joseph and my father signed this document, we were legally married. We were in the betrothal period, but nonetheless, we were married. As part of the Ketubbah, Joseph had to include all the promises he was making to me. The bridegroom would never take this lightly, as it is a legal document. Likewise, Jesus made numerous promises to his disciples and followers, to his bride. We can surely expect that he will carry through with each and every promise. I look forward to seeing every one of them come to fruition. Some of the promises I remember hearing Jesus say, as well as the ones his disciples have retold, are:

- *"Come to me, all you who are weary and burdened, and I will give you rest."*[33]
- *"I am the light of the world. Whoever follows me will never walk in darkness, but will have the light of life."*[34]

---

[33] Matthew 11:28 NIV
[34] John 8:12 NIV

- *"I am the resurrection and the life. The one who believes in me will live, even though they die; and whoever lives by believing in me will never die."*[35]
- *"But seek first his kingdom and his righteousness, and all these things will be given to you as well."*[36]
- *"If you hold to my teaching, you are really my disciples. Then you will know the truth, and the truth will set you free."*[37]
- *"Do not leave Jerusalem, but wait for the gift my Father promised, which you have heard me speak about. For John baptized with water, but in a few days you will be baptized with the Holy Spirit."*[38] This is one of the reasons we are meeting daily, waiting on God's Holy Spirit to arrive.

---

[35] John 11:25-26 NIV
[36] Matthew 6:33 NIV
[37] John 8:31-32 NIV
[38] Acts 1:4-5 NIV

- *"And surely I will be with you always, to the very end of the age."*[39] What an awesome promise; he will be with us forever!

Something else that happens during the Ketubbah period is the Mikvah, a ritual immersion into a pool. The Mikvah left me feeling so cleansed, a sort of purification, symbolically leaving my old life and entering my new life. Following the Mikvah, Joseph and I made our first public appearance under the Huppah (canopy) to announce our betrothal publicly. Such a joyous time! This sounds so much like what the disciples are teaching and performing in the name of Jesus—baptism, representing new birth, and a public profession of this new belief in Jesus.

The hardest part of our betrothal period was the Kiddushim, the set-apart period. Joseph and I were separated for a time. During this time, the bridegroom typically goes to prepare a home or to build a home for the couple. At this time, the couple is legally

---

[39] Matthew 28:20 NIV

married, but they cannot be physically together. No one really knows how long this will last. It is not the couple's decision; it is the decision of the bridegroom's father. The father decides when the new place is ready for them to inhabit. Jesus explained to his disciples that he was leaving to prepare a place for us and that he will return: *"I am going there to prepare a place for you ... And if I go and prepare a place for you, I will come back and take you to be with me that you also may be where I am."*[40] In addition to preparing a place for us, Jesus confirmed, *"But about that day or hour no one knows, not even the angels in heaven, nor the Son, but only the Father."*[41] God, the Father, will determine when Jesus, the Son, will return for his bride. I can't wait!

During this set-apart period, the bride spends a lot of time preparing herself for the return of her bridegroom. Some of the preparation effort is the actual making of the wedding garments. Some of John's teaching regarding Jesus as the bridegroom claims,

---

[40] John 14:2-3 NIV
[41] Mark 13:32 NIV

"the wedding of the Lamb has come, and his bride has made herself ready. Fine linen, bright and clean, was given her to wear. (Fine linen stands for the righteous acts of God's holy people.)."[42] The fine linen of Jesus' bride is the righteous acts of the believers. While Jesus is preparing a place for us, the preparation we are to be doing amounts to conducting righteous acts. It sounds like I've got some preparation work to do. It's probably best if I start by reflecting on the things Jesus taught, such as loving God and loving our neighbor.

Prior to going away, the bridegroom typically gives a bridal gift, the Matan, to his betrothed. This gift was a constant reminder to me of Joseph's love for me and his pledge to return for me. This is very similar to what we are now experiencing with Jesus. He told us he was sending the gift of the Holy Spirit to be our Comforter. We are expecting the arrival of the Holy Spirit any day now. We will have the gift of the Holy Spirit as our constant reminder of Jesus in our lives.

---

[42] Revelation 19:7-8 NIV

During the Kiddushim, the set-apart period, the couple is literally separated from each other, but they are also separated from other potential suitors. They have made a commitment to each other and are to focus on preparing for their time together. During the Kiddushim, my focus was on Joseph, my bridegroom, and no one else. I was preparing myself for his return to take me as his bride. This sounds so similar to what God told Moses, saying we are to be holy because He set us apart to be His own. God set us apart, and now His Son has gone to prepare a place for us. I've heard the disciples talk about Jesus' prayer in which he prayed that God would sanctify us; this was just another way of saying to make us holy, separated from the world. We are to be separated from anyone or anything that would prevent us from being prepared for Jesus' return. Already I am so longing for Jesus' return!

When Joseph's father decided it was the Nissuin, the time for Joseph to return to get his bride, it was quite a celebration. No one knew exactly when it was going to begin. We had a suspicion it was getting close, but since we didn't know, we just had to be ready. I did everything I could imagine to be ready. I was so excited! In keeping with the tradition, the processional began with the sounding of the Shofar (a ram's horn), and then one of my attendants shouted, *Behold, the bridegroom comes!* A long festival of celebration began, and at the end of the celebration, we were married. Similarly, Jesus told us of the announcement that will be made upon his return: *"When they see the Son of Man coming on the clouds of heaven, with power and great glory. And he will send his angels with a loud trumpet call, and they will gather his elect."*[43] The Son of Man, Jesus, the bridegroom, will return when his Father says, and it will be announced with a trumpet call—the Shofar. We best be ready.

Marriage is such a great comparison of our relationship to Jesus, of the relationship between Christ and his church. It is such a perfect analogy. Why didn't I see it when Jesus was with us? Joseph was a great husband, but he was not perfect. It's very evident to me

---

[43] Matthew 24:30-31 NIV

that Jesus will be the perfect bridegroom to his bride, his church. I so look forward to that day.

Messianic Prophecies

While we wait on the arrival of the Holy Spirit, we've also been reminding each other about the Messianic prophecies that were written by the prophets of old, prophecies that were fulfilled by Jesus. The Jewish leaders obviously didn't see Jesus as the fulfillment of the Messianic prophecies. In fact, I'm not sure any of us saw it either, at least not while Jesus was with us. It is a lot easier to look back in order to put the pieces of the puzzle together, the pieces presented by so many different prophets so long ago.

The prophet Isaiah exclaimed the impossible: *"The virgin will conceive and give birth to a son."*[44] A young lady, who never had marital relations, was to have a baby. How this was possible was beyond imagination. That virgin was me, chosen by God, to carry His Son, to raise His Son. The God of the universe chose me. I was

---
[44] Isaiah 7:14 NIV

so humbled and honored and excited – all at the same time. I also had no comprehension of what it meant. I'm now wondering if I will ever truly grasp what has happened. I just wanted to please God, to serve Him, to obey Him. I always wanted that, and I still do. The recent events have only heightened my desire to please God.

The prophet Micah declared where the Messiah would be born: *"But you, Bethlehem Ephrathah, though you are small among the clans of Judah, out of you will come for me one who will be ruler over Israel, whose origins are from of old, from ancient times."*[45] It's not like we planned to have our baby born in Bethlehem. I was very late in my pregnancy when the decree was issued that everyone had to return to their hometown so a census could be taken of the entire Roman world. Bethlehem, the town of David, was where we had to go. Jesus was born while we were there. It appears God used Caesar Augustus to cause this prophecy to come true: it was part of His plan.

---

[45] Micah 5:2 NIV

The prophet Jeremiah told everyone that God said the Messiah would be a descendant of King David by stating, *"The days are coming when I will raise up for David a righteous Branch, a King who will reign wisely and do what is just and right in the land."*[46] There is no doubt Jesus is of the lineage of David, as both my family and Joseph's have descended from David. Obviously, there are lots of other people who are descendants of David, but they cannot lay claim to the other prophecies as well.

I wonder if anyone believed the prophet Hosea when he proclaimed God's Son would be called out of Egypt: *"When Israel was a child, I loved him, and out of Egypt I called my son."*[47] After all, God's Son would be of Hebrew descent and would naturally be coming out of the land of Israel. However, when Herod was looking to kill baby Jesus, God's angel sent us to Egypt. When it was safe to return home, we were called out of Egypt by another of God's

---

[46] Jeremiah 23:5 NIV
[47] Hosea 11:1 NIV

angels. This journey had not been in our plans. Joseph and I had never talked about making a trip to Egypt.

The prophet Zechariah announced how the king would approach the city: *"See, your king comes to you, righteous and victorious, lowly and riding on a donkey, on a colt, the foal of a donkey."*[48] This would have been quite contrary to anyone's expectations of a king. Everyone was expecting a warrior king riding on a stately horse, who would save his people, but that obviously wasn't who Jesus was. It was just a few weeks ago that Jesus rode a donkey along the road to Jerusalem, as the people shouted, *"Blessed is he who comes in the name of the Lord,"*[49] as was predicted by the psalmist long ago. It's too bad the crowds of people didn't recognize Jesus as their King, the King they had been expecting.

---

[48] Zechariah 9:9 NIV
[49] Psalm 118:26 NIV

The prophet Isaiah told how the Messiah would not be accepted by men but rather *"despised and rejected by mankind, a man of sorrows, and familiar with pain."*[50] Could there be any greater rejection than what Jesus received? He was all about loving and serving others. It was never about himself. However, not only was he arrested, but after all the good he did, the people rejected him by having a convicted murderer released in exchange for Jesus to be crucified. Pure rejection! I know Jesus is alive, but it still brings me to tears when I think back on that horrific couple of days in which they tortured him—totally causing so much pain and rejection.

Not only did strangers reject Jesus, but King David foretold of a close and trusted friend who would betray the Messiah by saying, *"Even my close friend, someone I trusted, one who shared my bread, has turned against me."*[51] What was Judas Iscariot thinking? Was he planning this all along, or was it some last-minute

---

[50] Isaiah 53:3 NIV
[51] Psalm 41:9 NIV

temptation that corrupted him enough to assist in Jesus' death? We now know it was part of God's plan, but I still can't imagine what Judas was thinking. Jesus loved him!

King David wrote a lot of prophecies about the Messiah, about Jesus. He foretold how Jesus would escape one of the usual parts of the crucifixion process when he said that *"he protects all his bones, not one of them will be broken."*[52] I was so relieved when the soldiers did not break Jesus' bones, but at the time, I had no idea about the significance of that action. I wonder how long it will take to fully understand all that Jesus did, all that he was, and all that he taught? His disciples are now teaching that Jesus was the Lamb of God, the sacrifice that was needed to save us all from our sins. That's some heavy stuff for a mother to contemplate about her son. In support of what David wrote, Moses taught regarding the Passover Lamb that *"they must not ... break any of its bones."*[53] Was the purpose of that teaching to help us better understand the

---

[52] Psalm 34:20 NIV
[53] Numbers 9:12 NIV

significance behind Jesus' life, death, and resurrection as the lamb of God? David's broken bones prophecy seems so insignificant until understanding Moses' teaching about the sacrificial lamb. Jesus was the Sacrificial Lamb of God, and his bones were not broken. Even though the breaking of prisoner's bones is normal during the crucifixion process, hundreds of years before Jesus' death, God knew that his bones would not be broken.

We now recognize so many of the ancient prophecies that came true with Jesus. I can't wait to learn about more of the prophecies that have been fulfilled, but what about the ones that haven't yet come true? In addition to what the prophets foretold, Jesus also said things about his return that we can now seriously believe with all expectation. The disciples are talking about all that is still to come. They sure have me wondering what's next; what can we expect?

Knowing what I now know, I doubt there are many Jewish leaders who thought very highly of what the prophet Isaiah stated, that the Messiah would be *"a light for the Gentiles."*[54] What does this really mean? Was Jesus here for their benefit as well? He didn't seem to care who he helped. It wasn't always the Hebrew people that he helped. According to what the disciples claimed, much to everyone's surprise, he had compassion on a Samaritan woman at a well in Samaria. No other rabbi would have done that. No other rabbi would have ever considered walking through Samaria, let alone be seen talking with a Samaritan woman. Jesus was unlike any other, and he really stirred things up during his time on this earth. I can't imagine the chaos that will develop when the disciples start reaching out to the Gentile people. Will the disciples be subject to being killed as well for such radical teaching as welcoming Gentiles?

Jesus promised he would send the Holy Spirit by saying, *"You will receive power when the Holy Spirit comes on you; and you will be my witnesses in Jerusalem, and in all Judea and Samaria, and*

---

[54] Isaiah 42:6 NIV

to the ends of the earth."[55] The Holy Spirit is to be our Comforter, as well as our strength when we go out and tell others (both Jews and Gentiles) about the redeeming love of Jesus. We are waiting and expecting the Holy Spirit any day now. I don't think we know what to expect, but we are anxious for the Holy Spirit's arrival.

When questioned about the timing of his return, Jesus said he would return when the Father determines it is appropriate. We don't know when he will return, but we sure hope it is soon. It is going to be quite a celebration on that day. Following his return will be our journey to heaven, eternity with Jesus! I sure am ready.

I wonder how long God was planning all of this. It surely was long enough to be able to make prophetic announcements, hundreds and even thousands of years before coming true. What an amazingly awesome God we serve!

---

[55] Acts 1:8 NIV

Looking Back at the Cross

During our time together, another topic of discussion we had regarded the external events that happened at the time of Jesus' death on the cross:

- The sun stopped shining for three hours
- The earth shook
- The temple curtain was torn in two.

The "why" of these events seems to have most people quite perplexed. When thinking back to those hours, my mind concludes—of course, what else would happen when the Son of God was unjustifiably killed? These events may have simply been a reaction to the immense pain and anguish suffered by God the Father, Creator of the Universe, at the heinous treatment and subsequent death of His Son.

For many centuries, there has been the Jewish tradition of tearing one's clothes when immense pain, grief, or anguish is encountered. There are many examples from our ancestors, which have been recorded. Jacob tore his clothes when he thought Joseph had been killed. David tore his clothes when he learned that Saul and Jonathan had been killed. Elisha did it when Elijah was taken up into heaven. Mordecai did it when he heard of Haman's plan to have the Jews killed. When the Israelite community refused to go into the Promised Land, Joshua and Caleb tore their clothes. There are more examples as well. Considering the Jewish people are God's chosen people, why wouldn't we expect a similar reaction by God, our Father, when his son is unjustifiably killed? Such intense pain the God of all Love must have experienced. As clothing keeps others from seeing our bodies, the temple curtain kept us from seeing God. It just makes so much sense to me that in His extreme grief, God would tear the curtain, just tear it in two, at the death of His Son.

Why wouldn't an earth-shaking reaction be expected as well, a God-sized response to the killing of His Son? I've heard of people hitting or throwing something when they've been angered or hurt in some way. Again, why wouldn't we expect such a reaction from the God of all Creation when such an atrocity is committed against His beloved Son, the Son who talked about a special oneness in their relationship. We now realize they had a relationship, unlike any relationship we can imagine. The shaking of the earth sounds just like what the prophet Jeremiah explained about God: *"When he is angry, the earth trembles."*[56] Could anything anger God more than the unconscionable killing of His Son? As such, an earthquake at the time of Jesus' death seems like a reaction we could expect from God, his Father.

Throughout the horrendous events of that day, I often closed my eyes. This was just a reaction to keep from seeing the awful things that were being done to Jesus. In effect, I was blocking the light from getting to my eyes. Did God block the light as well to keep from seeing the event, or even to keep others from seeing all that was happening? No matter how you look at it, it was a "dark" day. I'm also finding it interesting to ponder the words Jesus spoke

---

[56] Jeremiah 10:10 NIV

by saying, *"I am the light of the world."*[57] Think about it—the killing of Jesus snuffed out that light! In fact, those who were responsible for crucifying Jesus were truly walking in darkness, a spiritual darkness. But for a few hours, they also got a sample of physical darkness, a reflection of their lives to come.

That's just my thinking. The disciples are teaching something a bit different, especially regarding the tearing of the temple curtain. The curtain separated the Holy of Holies, God's dwelling place, from the rest of the temple. The rest of the temple is the meeting place for men and is the location for the daily sacrifices. The disciples are now teaching that Jesus was the final sacrifice, the final atonement for our sins. We no longer must make sin offerings, and the Holy of Holies is now open for all. We no longer need to have the high priest enter the Holy of Holies once a year on our behalf to make our sin offerings. Jesus is the way to God the Father. According to what John is telling everyone, Jesus said, *"I am the*

---

[57] John 8:12 NIV

way and the truth and the life. No one comes to the Father except through me."[58] Jesus is the only way to a relationship with God the Father! There's no longer a need for someone to go between us and God, no longer a need for the temple curtain. It is so simple, but I wonder how many people will miss the opportunity to have a personal relationship with Jesus and God the Father? Through such pain and suffering, Jesus made the way to God the Father very simple: just trust and believe in His Son, Jesus.

No matter what, the temple curtain was coming down. It was no longer needed to keep the people separated from God. However, it could have come down in many orderly ways, just like when it was originally hung in the temple. It was huge and very thick, and God destroyed it in a moment, at the death of His Son.

---

[58] John 14:6 NIV

Stories from the Disciples

As we continue meeting for prayer and encouragement, some of the disciples are recounting stories of their experiences, as well as their reactions to the adventures. Everyone has a story, but the biggest storytellers seem to be Matthew, Mark, Luke, and John, but as I think about it, Peter has quite a bit to tell as well. No matter who spent time with Jesus, it had an impact on their life.

Peter is excitedly telling everyone about an event, a story of which he and a couple of others were sworn to secrecy, at least *"until the Son of Man has been raised from the dead."*[59] On one particular day, Peter and a few others went with Jesus to the mountain to pray. However, while they were there, Jesus was transfigured right before their eyes. His clothes turned an amazing white, a white like Peter had never seen. In addition, Elijah and Moses were there, and Jesus talked with them. Not only that, Peter emphasized they heard a voice from heaven say, *"This is my Son,*

---

[59] Matthew 17:9 NIV

whom I love; with him, I am well pleased."[60] Peter is talking like it was the most amazing thing. It is amazing! He was so excited! That very day he wanted to tell others, but Jesus wouldn't let them tell anyone. Besides that, who would have believed that they saw Elijah and Moses? Maybe that's why Jesus didn't want them to tell others about the story; no one would believe them. However, considering the events of recent weeks, this story is now more than believable. No wonder it is one of the first stories Peter decided to tell.

You should hear the disciples tell about the night they were on a boat, crossing the lake. I've heard this story told many times. I just don't think they get tired of telling it. They had been very busy prior to getting into the boat, and all were exhausted. Jesus fell asleep nearly as soon as his head hit the pillow. No sooner was he asleep when a terrible storm came out of nowhere, totally unexpected. They describe it as having caused instant terror among all of them, everyone except Jesus. Keep in mind there were

---

[60] 2 Peter 1:17 NIV

seasoned fishermen on this boat–they were men who had been on a boat, on this lake, for most of their lives, having experienced many storms over the years. These men were also terrified, yet Jesus slept peacefully. In fear for their lives, they woke him. When Jesus awoke, he simply rebuked the storm, and it instantly calmed down. His mere words had power over the wind and the waves. This apparently left a boatful of men in utter amazement, wondering just who this Jesus is who has control over the weather. They thought they knew him, but apparently not as well as they thought.

Luke has been re-telling about the time they were all walking in a large crowd towards the house of Jairus. The crowd was so large it nearly felt like they were going to be crushed. Everyone in the crowd wanted to get close to Jesus. Luke remembers thinking, *it is a good thing none of us are claustrophobic.* Then, all of a sudden, they hear Jesus say, "Who *touched me?"*[61] They were all thinking, *what's he talking about? There's a huge crowd; of course, someone touched him.* There were many people who were touching him. It seemed like such a silly question to them. Peter was the one willing to speak up and ask Jesus why he was asking who touched him. Luke sensed a bit of sarcasm in Peter's voice. Apparently, Jesus sensed some healing power having been taken from him, something of which the disciples had no understanding. One person from the crowd, a lady who had been bleeding for years, was the one who reached out to touch Jesus for his healing power. None of the disciples had a clue what was going on until Jesus affirmed this woman and her faith. She was instantly healed because she had so much faith. Her faith really seemed to impress Jesus. I think it impressed the disciples as well.

There's another story regarding a boat and waves, told by Matthew. The disciples were crossing the Sea of Galilee one

---

[61] Luke 8:45 NIV

evening. They were not making much progress due to a strong headwind. As they were fighting the wind, someone spotted an apparition on the water. They were terrified at the thought of what it was. Then they heard the familiar voice of Jesus calling to them. Jesus was walking on water! He simply amazed the disciples more and more every day, often multiple times a day. According to Matthew, it wasn't enough for them just to be amazed. Peter, being the spontaneous person that he is, asked Jesus to invite him to join Jesus on the water! Everyone in the boat was either saying or thinking, *No, Peter, don't do it,* but he did it anyway. Apparently, he didn't stay on top of the water for very long, though. When he started to sink into the water, Jesus seemed to question Peter's faith. As I think about the situation, Peter may have taken his eyes off Jesus, but no one else suggested getting out of the boat to join Jesus. There must be a message in this story about joining Jesus wherever he is and not letting the seemingly impossible get in our way. I'm sure the disciples will talk about this for some time to come.

Many of the disciples are talking about the first time Jesus sent them out to preach the good news of God, to heal the sick, and to drive out demons. According to Luke, Jesus told them they are to *"take nothing for the journey – no staff, no bag, no bread, no money, no extra shirt."*[62] They talk about it being a bit unnerving at first. What were they going to do if no one offered them a place to stay or food to eat? They didn't even have an extra tunic which would have allowed them to be able to sleep outdoors if necessary. They really didn't understand (at the time) that they were to trust Jesus and to be obedient when he gave them something to do. It turned out to be a very successful journey—people heard the good news, people were healed, demons were cast out, and no disciple lacked food or a place to stay. It is clear it was a very invigorating experience, all because they were obedient, doing what Jesus said to do.

---

[62] Luke 9:3 NIV

All of them want to say something about the time Jesus told them to feed 5,000 people. Really it was around 5,000 men, plus the women and children who were with the men. There's no way Jesus wouldn't have also fed the women and children. Apparently, the disciples really thought Jesus was crazy, probably from spending too much time in the hot sun. They remember thinking that it was a lot of people to feed, even if they had the resources to do it, but all they had were just five loaves of bread and two fish. How could that feed 5,000? Apparently, Jesus didn't give it a second thought; he simply took the five loaves and two fish, gave thanks to God, and then told his disciples to distribute the food. The way the story is being told, it is easy to envision the disciples giving Jesus a look that said he was crazy—they still had just five loaves of bread and two fish. However, being obedient, they started distributing the food to the first group of people, and to the next group, and to the next, and the food never ran out. After all the people were satisfied, the disciples picked up 12 basketfuls of leftover food—one basket for each disciple! How can that possibly happen, aside from Jesus being the Son of God? According to Phillip's calculations, it would have taken at least eight months of someone's wages to be able to buy enough food for everyone in attendance. Jesus merely gave thanks, and the food was provided—enough to fill everyone and to have leftovers. The disciples were in awe when they realized what was done in their presence. It's obvious they are still in awe over this one.

It doesn't seem like there are as many disciples willing to retell the story of Jesus instructing them to feed 4,000 men. Matthew was willing to tell the story, with a little help from Mark, but not with the same enthusiasm as when they told about feeding the 5,000. They seem to be a bit ashamed that they asked Jesus, *"where could we get enough bread in this remote place to feed such a crowd?"*[63] This event occurred just a short time after they witnessed Jesus feeding 5,000 with such a small amount of food. In fact, they had a bit more food to start with this time. They were

---

[63] Matthew 15:33 NIV

ashamed because they had recently seen Jesus perform a very similar miracle, and they did not seem to remember what they had experienced or who was telling them to feed the people. The common thought among them goes something like how disappointed Jesus must have been with each of them at times, as no matter how many miracles he performed, there was still a bit of disbelief. I think we can all relate to that statement.

According to John, sometimes they were completely dumbfounded, not knowing what to say and afraid of asking seemingly stupid questions. He remembers the time they found Jesus talking with the Samaritan woman at the well. They were all surprised because a Jew doesn't talk with Samaritans, especially Samaritan women. Jesus sure violated that unwritten rule of no talking with Samaritans. They all wanted to ask him about the encounter, but no one was brave enough to ask. They didn't want to be criticized the way Jesus criticized the Pharisees. After all, the Pharisees were supposedly much more knowledgeable in matters about God, or so they wanted everyone to believe. The disciples were still in training, under the teaching of Jesus, and of course, who wants to sound stupid in front of their teacher? This was no exception. Unfortunately, they all now understand how much more they would have learned if only they had been daring enough to ask. After all, asking questions is one of the best ways of learning.

John had a bit of a grin on his face when he told how Nathanael (also called Bartholomew) had the best foot-in-mouth comment when he first heard about Jesus. Apparently, as soon as Philip told him about Jesus, Nathanael simply said, *"Nazareth! Can anything good come from there?"*[64] He was also heard saying a good recovery statement just a short while later: *"Rabbi, you are the Son of God; you are the king of Israel."*[65] Upon meeting Jesus, it was obvious to everyone there was something different about him and, yes, something good could come out of Nazareth. I wonder how many stupid things each of us said about Jesus before we really

---

[64] John 1:46 NIV
[65] John 1:49 NIV

got to know him? I'm sure more than just the twelve had the opportunity to say something they later regretted.

Every time I think there couldn't be any more stories, someone else brings up another experience they had with Jesus. Someone suggested, I think it was John, that *"Jesus did many other things as well. If every one of them were written down, I suppose that even the whole world would not have room for the books that would be written."*[66] At that point, another story began.

Peter started to tell about the time Jesus washed their feet. That single act by Jesus really made quite an impression on Peter. At first, Peter was very opposed to Jesus washing his feet as that was one of the dirtiest, lowliest tasks a servant could do for their master. Peter wanted nothing to do with having his Lord wash his feet. Once Jesus explained he was demonstrating what he wanted his disciples to do, basically, to be servant leaders, Peter was on board with the concept. It is still a very different approach from

---

[66] John 21:25 NIV

what any other leader has taught, but isn't everything Jesus taught very different than the norm?

There must have been a number of the disciples present when the young, rich man approached Jesus and basically asked what he needed to do to get into heaven. I say that because a lot of them commented about the look on that young man's face when Jesus told him to *"go, sell everything you have and give to the poor, and you will have treasure in heaven. Then come, follow me."*[67] Apparently, that young man was shocked by the response and was not ready for that kind of commitment—to give everything to follow Jesus. I'm sure we all hold onto something from our past, but hopefully, each day, we are giving up more and more of our past to follow Jesus—making him completely Lord of our lives.

Apparently, Peter, James, and John (brother of James) were with Jesus when he raised a young girl, I think only about 12 years old, from the dead. It was obvious to everyone at the house the girl

---

[67] Mark 10:21 NIV

was dead. It was so obvious to them that they laughed when Jesus claimed she was just sleeping. All Jesus did was speak to the girl, and she got up—such a miracle, yet Jesus would not let them tell anyone about it. Why? Why wouldn't he want others to know what he did, what he could do? This seemed to be a common instruction Jesus had when he did a miracle for people—*"don't tell anyone."* Maybe the crowds that followed him were already too large, and if word spread about all the miracles, the crowds would grow even larger. It is still not always obvious to me why Jesus did or said certain things. I'm still learning.

It makes me, the mother of Jesus, so excited to hear people tell the stories of their time with Jesus. Many of these stories I had not previously heard. Just sharing among ourselves, we are learning more and more each day about Jesus and him being the Son of God, but I also know he is the child I bore and raised. With that in mind, I'm thoroughly enjoying hearing more and more about my son. This time together with other believers is invaluable to me.

I had heard about the festive celebration as Jesus approached Jerusalem, less than a week before he was crucified, where the crowds placed branches and coats on the ground. What I find additionally interesting is the story being told about what happened just prior to his entry into Jerusalem. Jesus told a couple of his disciples to *"go to the village ahead of you, and as you enter it, you will find a colt tied there, which no one has ever ridden. Untie it and bring it here. If anyone asks you, 'Why are you untying it?' say, 'The Lord needs it.'"*[68] Some of them seemed to suggest they felt like they were stealing, or at least wondered if the donkey's owner would think they were stealing the donkey. Strange how the owners had no problem with them taking the donkey after the disciples said what Jesus had told them to say. Jesus sure had different approaches to situations, but he never led them astray. Everything Jesus told was the truth, and he would never suggest stealing anything.

---

[68] Luke 19:30-31 NIV

Most of the stories that have been told include a bit of fondness for the storyteller, or at least there is some lesson included which can now be better understood, but there are a couple of stories that seem to be very difficult to tell. It is obvious they just cut to the innermost of the person, making it almost impossible for them to retell. You can see them experience the event all over again as they talk about it.

One such event occurred shortly after Jesus was arrested. Peter, almost as a confession, tells how he followed the soldiers who had arrested Jesus. It is still difficult to hear about that event but also difficult for him to articulate. The most difficult part of the story for Peter to discuss was when he was in the courtyard of the high priest, and he was questioned three times about his relationship with Jesus. Each time he denied knowing Jesus. Not only was Jesus the man whom Peter emphatically exclaimed was *"the Messiah, the Son of the living God,"*[69] but he was also

---

[69] Matthew 16:16 NIV

reminded of when Jesus predicted that he would deny him three times. Peter felt so horrible. You can see tears well up as he tells the story. He felt like such a hypocrite. When things were good, he could proclaim Jesus as Lord; but when things were going wrong, he couldn't even admit he knew him. The other disciples did come a bit to his defense. They also felt ashamed of their actions following Jesus' arrest—they ran and hid. From their perspective, at least Peter tried to stay close to Jesus, not running in the other direction. Not one of the twelve fully grasped the fullness of Jesus; no one did. Things have surely changed since Jesus' resurrection. Such a boldness the disciples now have, as well as a desire to tell the world about Jesus, with no fear.

When the disciples talk about the day Jesus was arrested, there are many stories just from that one day. That day must be permanently planted in their minds. Some great memories and some not so great. How could that not be the case? For three years, they did everything together. There were good times, bad times, exhilarating times, sad times, stressful times, scary times. You name it, and they likely experienced it together.

After having a great meal with Jesus, along with some teaching and singing of hymns, he took them to Gethsemane, a place he would often go to pray. Jesus wanted his disciples to be with him, but he also wanted to be alone while he prayed. Apparently, he told them not to fall asleep, to stay awake. And yet, each time he left them to go pray, the disciples fell asleep. They felt awful that they were unable to stay awake while he prayed, but they just could not do anything about it. As they talk among themselves, they have started to realize what an extremely busy schedule they'd had the previous several days. From the first day of the week until Jesus' arrest, there was a constant stream of activities:

- The parade and celebration were going into Jerusalem. As exhilarating as such an event can be, it can also be very exhausting.

- Jesus turning over the tables in the temple was a very emotional ordeal, leaving all the disciples wondering if they would all be arrested.

- Jesus, and the disciples, often stayed with Mary, Martha, and their brother Lazarus in Bethany, when they were in the Jerusalem area. It's about a two-mile walk each way, so they did a lot of walking those days.

- There was a lot of teaching happening during those days, from the fig tree lesson for the disciples to numerous crowd situations where Jesus taught using many parables. There may have been more parables taught in those few days than in Jesus' complete ministry. That intense learning environment was also very tiring.

- There were many discussions between Jesus and the crowds and with various authorities. Even though the direct encounters were with Jesus, these encounters were always emotionally exhausting for his companions.

- From the way they talk, it sounds like Thursday was a day that Jesus spent time alone with his disciples, but it doesn't sound like it was a day of rest. There were Passover preparations to be made as well as more teaching by Jesus.

The disciples were just exhausted from the very busy schedule they had kept. I wonder how exhausted Jesus must have been. By the time it was evening, when Jesus wanted to pray, as soon as the disciples closed their eyes, they just instantly fell asleep. Hopefully, they don't feel too bad. I'm sure Jesus understood. There really was no way for them to know what was about to happen.

And now it sounds like there is another story about to be told.

Peter is telling of when he made the decision to follow Jesus. He enjoys telling this story much more than the ones that seem to be about his failed attempts to follow Jesus. Jesus had used Peter's boat as a place to teach from when a large crowd surrounded him at the Sea of Galilee. After the teaching session was over, Jesus suggested that Peter go out into deeper waters and let down his nets. Even though Peter had just fished these waters and knew with confidence there were no fish to catch, he did what Jesus said. Amazingly, he caught more fish than he could manage. He had to call another boat to come and help. It was at that point Peter decided to leave the life he knew, to follow Jesus.

I'm confident these guys could talk forever about their adventures with Jesus. I'm sure I'll continue hearing more about my son, but for now, we are praying together while we await the coming of the Holy Spirit.

Chapter 5: The Holy Spirit

Wow! We knew the Holy Spirit was coming, but we really had no idea what to expect. I don't think anyone had the slightest clue as to what to expect. How could we? There's never been anything like it ever before. Jesus promised it would come but never mentioned what it would be like to experience it. For days we had been waiting, fellowshipping, praying, and talking, but we were really caught off guard when we heard the noise that only could be described as the strongest wind I had ever heard. It was amazing. We were instantly filled with the Holy Spirit! We were even speaking in other languages, and there were small flames of fire on us—fire that didn't burn. As I think about it, it makes me remember the burning bush as experienced by Moses. God's presence was seen through the fire, though it did not consume the bush. Likewise, the Holy Spirit came upon us in flames of fire but did not burn us.

Since our experience with the Holy Spirit, the disciples' focus has changed significantly. They are extremely intent on telling the world about their Savior, Jesus. As Peter puts it: *"Everyone who calls on the name of the Lord will be saved,"*[70] and he intends to do his part to make this happen. The Holy Spirit's indwelling of the disciples has given them a boldness for taking the message to the world, as Jesus had instructed them to do when he said, *"Go and make disciples of all nations, baptizing them in the name of the Father and of the Son and of the Holy Spirit, and teaching them to obey everything I have commanded you."*[71]

His disciples are very changed men since Jesus' resurrection. They have a joy that is unexplainable. For the years they were with Jesus, you could see a sense of contentment, but now there is joy— pure joy. What a blessing for them. Not only that, I can see in their

---

[70] Acts 2:21 NIV
[71] Matthew 28:19-20 NIV

actions the new boldness they have obtained. They are going to do great things in the name of Jesus.

All our lives have been changed for eternity. It is now our job to tell others about the amazing saving grace of the Lord Jesus Christ and that they can live for eternity with God if they only believe in his Son, Jesus!

What really amazes me, after all the time I've spent remembering the events of the last 32 or so years, is how badly I missed what God had made so visible to me. I truly hope others are more observant and can see that God sent His Son to earth to save us from our sins. I'm just blown away, considering God chose me to be the mother of the Lord Jesus, our Messiah. As he chose me, he will surely choose others to be a part of his master plan. It was not an easy task, being the mother of Jesus, and there are likely more difficult days ahead. However, there is one thing I am assured of for myself as well as others. When going through difficult times, even if

I don't immediately recognize it, God has a plan, and he is in control.

As mentioned earlier, I've not always known or believed in this hope we now have in Jesus, the hope of eternal life that he promises to those who love him and seek him. I did not understand this hope at the time when some folks thought I should be stoned as an adulterer, or when Herod was trying to kill Jesus, or when we lost Jesus for several days, or when cousin John was beheaded. I definitely didn't understand it when Jesus hung on the cross. No, there was no hope of any sort in me at those times. However, because of Jesus' resurrection and the indwelling of the Holy Spirit, I am now full of hope in Christ and want to tell others about it, just as Peter is telling us to *"always be prepared to give an answer to everyone who asks you to give the reason for the hope that you have."*[72]

---

[72] 1 Peter 3:15 NIV

It is now my desire for everyone to understand that Jesus, my son, the Son of God, died for our sins, was buried and was resurrected from the dead, so that everyone who believes in him will live with Jesus forever, in heaven.

Epilogue

How could Mary have ever imagined what future events and activities and hardships and joys were waiting for her following her initial encounter with the angel Gabriel? She likely considered many things and might even have thought she really grasped what had been told to her, but not until Christ's resurrection and the coming of the Holy Spirit could she have ever known what God was really planning.

Most likely, Mary thought her life was well planned out by her father, her future husband, and future father-in-law. There wasn't much else for her to do, or so she thought. Then came an unexpected visit from an angel, and all those plans were gone. Well, she still married Joseph, but who would have suggested that the rest of her experiences could possibly be planned out by a mere mortal man? She could not have imagined the intense roller coaster ride that raising the Son of God would present. The one and only thing that could have gotten her through those years of extreme ups and downs is the condition and attitude of her heart, as she stated, *"I am the Lord's servant."*[73] Mary was truly a woman of God.

Just as Mary had no idea of her journey following the visit of the angel Gabriel, she surely had no idea of the tumultuous events that would be encountered following Jesus' ascension. The one thing she surely learned up until that point was that she could trust God for His plan and wisdom and provision. That most likely is what would have gotten her through her remaining years as a first-century Christian, as a member of "The Way."

Following Christ's resurrection and ascension, life did not automatically get easier for Christ's followers. In fact, quite the opposite occurred. We are told in the first few chapters of the book of Acts that:

- Peter and John were arrested
- The Apostles were arrested, flogged, and threatened
- Stephen was stoned to death

---

[73] Luke 1:38 NIV

- The church (a.k.a. The Way) was persecuted, and people were scattered

- People were dragged out of their houses and placed into prisons

This is just a small sampling of the persecution that was immediately experienced by Believers—Christ Followers. As tradition has it and is recorded by historians of the time, it is believed that eleven of the twelve disciples were killed for their faith in Jesus. John, the twelfth disciple, was exiled to the island of Patmos because of his faith in Christ.

There really is no way to think that Mary was immune to the persecution that was going on all around her. The persecution was against the entire church, against all believers. Surely as his mother, Mary would have been included in the persecution. At the very least, she would have known of and witnessed firsthand the persecution of her friends, as well as the disciples of Jesus.

It can be discouraging to know that Jesus' immediate followers, and likely his mother, were persecuted. It can also be a bit disheartening when hearing that Jesus confirmed this by saying, *"Whoever wants to be my disciple must deny themselves and take up their cross daily and follow me."*[74] But it is encouraging that we have hope in the saving grace of the Lord Jesus when we believe and trust in him.

As believers in Christ, we are not immune to trials, hardships, or suffering of any kind, but we do have the promise from God that says, *"Never will I leave you; never will I forsake you."*[75] We also have a promise that God has a plan: *"For I know the plans I have for you ... plans to prosper you and not to harm you, plans to give you hope and a future."*[76] All we need to do is to trust and obey Him.

---

[74] Luke 9:23 NIV
[75] Hebrews 13:5 NIV
[76] Jeremiah 29:11 NIV

If you don't yet know Christ as your Lord and Savior, take a moment now to ask God to forgive you of your sins, to thank Him for sending Jesus to die for you, and to ask Him to live in you, to be Lord of your life.

Saying such a prayer won't make your difficulties go away, but you will look at them differently, and you will have the God of the Universe walking along beside you as you navigate the challenges of life.

Following Jesus' arrest, the disciples all ran from the situation or simply denied knowing Jesus for fear of their lives. In a very short amount of time, they went from being full of fear to being filled with the Holy Spirit and having a relentless boldness to preach the saving grace of the Lord Jesus Christ. No matter what they had previously encountered, it was all behind them. They were moving forward with Christ. I suspect that Mary would have been right along with the disciples in having a boldness to live for Christ. Likewise, no matter what we have experienced throughout our lives, God wants us to know He loves us and that he sent his Son to die for us, to save us from our sins. All he asks in return is that we love him and accept his Son as Lord of our lives.

About the Author

Kevin is a graduate of Grove City College, class of 1981, where he earned his bachelor's degree in Mechanical Engineering. Kevin's work career has given him many roles and responsibilities in manufacturing while living and working in the USA and Europe. He is currently president and co-owner of a business in Kittery, Maine: PTE Precision Machining. Kevin has two daughters, both of whom were recently married. After losing his first wife, Diane, to breast cancer, Kevin married his current wife, Pam, and instantly gained four sons, now with two daughters-in-law and two grandchildren. Besides time with his family, Kevin has always enjoyed various outdoor activities: water skiing, snow skiing, hiking, kayaking, canoeing, and traveling. In addition to his family and working career, Kevin has had a variety of roles within the various churches he and his family have attended. Kevin has had many serving opportunities, including both local opportunities and international short-term mission trips. However, of all the roles he has held within the church, the preparation and leading of small group Bible studies has brought him the most joy.